The Pioneer Woman Cooks
THE NEW FRONTIER

The Pioneer Woman Cooks
THE NEW FRONTIER

112 FANTASTIC FAVORITES FOR EVERYDAY EATING

REE DRUMMOND

WILLIAM MORROW
An Imprint of HarperCollinsPublishers

ALSO BY REE DRUMMOND

The Pioneer Woman Cooks: Recipes from an Accidental Country Girl

The Pioneer Woman Cooks: Food from My Frontier

The Pioneer Woman Cooks: A Year of Holidays

The Pioneer Woman Cooks: Dinnertime

The Pioneer Woman Cooks: Come and Get It!

The Pioneer Woman: Black Heels to Tractor Wheels—A Love Story

Charlie the Ranch Dog

Charlie and the Christmas Kitty

Charlie Goes to School

Charlie and the New Baby

Charlie Plays Ball

Little Ree

HarperCollins books may be purchased for educational, business, or sales promotional use. For information, please email the Special Markets Department at SPsales@harpercollins.com.

FIRST EDITION

Designed by Kris Tobiassen of Matchbook Digital

All food photographs by Ree Drummond

All other photographs by Ree Drummond except page iii by Buff Strickland; page viii center left by Alex Drummond, top right by Ladd Drummond, and lower right by Debbie Formby; page viii center right and page 83 fiesta by Ashley Alexander; page x by Paige Drummond; page xii upper left by Kevin Miyazaki; page xviii, page 101 P-Town sign, and page 301 Merc sign by Betsy Dutcher

Library of Congress Cataloging-in-Publication Data has been applied for.

ISBN 978-0-06-256137-4

19 20 21 22 23   WOR   10 9 8 7 6 5 4 3 2 1

To Alex, Paige, Bryce, and Todd

You're the center of my frontier, and I love you so much.

—MOM

Contents

Introduction
IT'S A NEW FRONTIER 'ROUND HERE!

Hi, friends! I can't tell you how excited I am to share this cookbook with you. It represents a whole lot of passion—about the food I love to cook, the food I *reallllly* love to eat, and the food I'm serving my family and friends.

It also represents a lot of changes. For the first time since my husband, Ladd, and I started our family (twenty-three years ago! How is that possible?), our household has experienced quite a noticeable shift. Alex, our oldest child, graduated from college. Paige, our second, left for college (and not, by the way, without weeks of tears from her mother). That left Ladd and me at home with our two teenage sons, and the four of us have been assimilating and navigating a whole new dynamic at home.

And what a dynamic it's been! Bryce and Todd are high school athletes, so if they aren't training for football season, they're at all-day wrestling tournaments or track meets. Last summer marked the onset of serious football camps for Bryce, who has two more years of high school. Meantime, Ladd is a full-time rancher, but he's also a dedicated sports dad and helps facilitate a lot of the logistics involved with the boys' sports. All of this means

that I am basically residing in a man cave that's either echoing from emptiness (because they're at practice or working on the ranch) or buzzing like a cafeteria (because when they're home, all they want to do is eat). There is very little idle talk around the dinner table about the varied topics my girls and I used to fill the air with; nowadays, it's all boy, all sports, all stats, all dirty clothes, all the time. And then they go to bed and it starts all over again the next morning.

Fortunately, I happen to be a glass-is-half-full optimist, so I have learned to embrace the positive side of this brand-new reality in the Drummond family. With fewer humans in the house, still, quiet moments are a little easier to come by than they once were. The laundry's a little lighter, the clutter's a little more manageable, and I'm able to achieve a little more momentum with my work because of the longer stretches of alone time! I'm able to take more photos of the ranching and the animals, and while I still feel like every day is as busy as it can possibly be, I'm actually starting to feel like I have a fighting chance of staying on top of my to-do list. (When all four kids were in the house, anything I ever accomplished had to have been purely accidental. I don't know how I got anything done!)

This has also allowed me more time to work with Ladd on continuing to dig in our roots in

grew up, and we hope to have at least some of our kids back here one day.

On the kitchen front (my favorite part!), this change in our household has afforded me more time to think about food, to crave, to create and plan meals, and to experiment with new foods and methods that excite me. Oh, I'm still cooking every day as always, despite the shift in our family's routine, but it most certainly feels like a new frontier in my kitchen in so many ways.

What does a "new frontier" look like? For me, it means fresh, new recipes, but it also means ingredients I haven't used before (Halloumi, see page 254). It might mean a different approach to meal prep, to reflect the changing needs and schedules of my family. Some days it might mean a new take on an old favorite recipe (Lower-Carb Eggs Benedict, page 47) or using a new piece of equipment to make an old favorite recipe (Instant Pot Short Rib Pot Roast, page 199). Or it might mean mashing up two previously unrelated dishes (Buffalo Chicken Quesadillas, page 145) and making something new.

It definitely feels like a new frontier in my kitchen when I use store-bought versions of ingredients I once made entirely from scratch (example: balsamic glaze; I never make my own anymore because it's readily available to buy) . . . or when I make ingredients from scratch that I only used to buy (teriyaki sauce, see page 272). It might mean having some international fun by clashing continents in the same recipe (Greek Guacamole, page 92) . . . or by mixing up levels of elegance by using high-quality puff pastry to wrap cocktail wieners (see page 114)! And, to

Pawhuska. After opening The Mercantile in 2016, we have gradually added a small (just eight rooms!) hotel, a pizza restaurant, and an ice cream store. Being able to set up shop in our small town holds a lot of meaning for us, as it's the place where Ladd reflect the current state of watch-your-waistline trends, it might mean putting lower carb spins on recipes one week, then throwing it all out the window the next week—or, heck, sometimes the very same day! (I don't do well with self-denial.)

Page 177

Page 254

Page 242

Page 89

Page 185

Page 81

Page 161

Page 111

Page 321

This new frontier in my kitchen is about having the freedom to have fun and to spread my cooking wings . . . but it's also about appreciating that some things never need to change, like comforting chicken and dumplings (page 147), Ladd's all-time favorite pasta (page 185) that I've made for him since we were first married, and good ol' decadent doughnuts (page 321). As much as I love tasty new recipes and putting new spins on old classics, I know how important it is to keep the well-loved dishes familiar and unaltered.

This has been more relevant over the past two years than ever, because we lost Ladd's beloved mom, Nan. She was a grandmother, mother, mother-in-law, and good friend. Her death was a new territory our family wasn't prepared for, and we have learned to cling to memories and traditions, both in and out of the kitchen. Since she was so relevant in our daily lives, from small everyday gatherings to big celebrations, it's been a difficult adjustment for all of us. We sure do miss her every day.

Life goes on, and it is ever changing. Just when you settle into a routine and have it all figured out, things evolve and you have to adjust. But for all the changes, I am consciously and fully embracing this new frontier I'm in. It's definitely uncharted for me, but there is so much to love and be grateful for every day . . . and change is a part of life. And I'm sure going to breathe in and enjoy . . . because I know in a few years, the picture will be totally different!

I hope you love and enjoy this cookbook, friends. It's filled with all the delicious kinds of food we all know and love, but with some great spins and surprises here and there. I enjoyed cooking every recipe (and photographing them, too—my camera is a mess!), and I hope they become a regular part of your own frontier.

Lots of love,

Ree

Equipment in This Book

All things considered, the equipment used in this book is pretty simple! Here's a brief explanation of my essentials.

Nonstick skillet

WHAT: A lightweight skillet with a baked-on nonstick coating.

WHEN: For making fuss-free eggs, omelets, French toast, and simple skillet dinners.

WHY: It makes cooking and cleanup a breeze!

WHY NOT: Coating wears off over time. Also, high heat isn't recommended, which makes searing and frying difficult.

Cast-iron skillet

WHAT: A tough-as-nails skillet made of solid cast iron.

WHEN: For searing meats, cooking pizza, frying chicken, or anytime you need high heat.

WHY: It won't dent or break, you can't hurt it, and it lasts forever. You can cook on the stovetop or in the oven.

WHY NOT: It's very heavy, especially when filled with food. It can also be difficult to reduce the heat quickly since the iron retains heat so well.

Dutch oven

WHAT: A round (or oval), heavy-duty pot with a lid. Often made of cast iron and coated with enamel.

WHEN: For making stews, soups, and pot roasts, and for deep frying.

WHY: It's extremely versatile and very durable! It's perfect for stovetop-to-oven cooking because you can cook and serve in the same vessel.

WHY NOT: It can be extremely heavy, especially when filled with food.

Sheet pan

WHAT: A commercial "half sheet" (13 x 18-inch) stainless cake pan that has become a kitchen staple in both professional and home kitchens.

WHEN: For baking cookies, cakes, or brownies; cooking bacon or other meats in the oven; or roasting meats and vegetables. (Tip: I use sheet pans as lids for skillets in a pinch!)

WHY: It's endlessly versatile, very inexpensive, and very durable.

WHY NOT: The basic pans are best but are usually available only in restaurant supply stores. (This is the only con I can think of! I'm a sheet pan fan.)

Slow cooker

WHAT: A countertop appliance designed for cooking low and (hence the name) slow.

WHEN: For making all-day soups, stews, roasts, and casseroles. It can be used as a makeshift chafing dish for queso at a party.

WHY: It's very convenient and fuss-free; just throw in the ingredients, turn it on, and go about your day. It's also helpful in the hot summer, when you don't want to turn on the oven.

WHY NOT: You can't brown anything in a slow cooker; searing requires a separate step in a skillet on the stove. It's sometimes hard to control texture and develop flavors because everything goes in at once.

Instant Pot

WHAT: A countertop appliance with multiple uses, the most notable being a pressure cooker. (Other uses are a slow cooker, yogurt maker, and more.)

WHEN: For long-braising meats like pot roasts or briskets (they cook in a fraction of the time), soups, pulled pork, and hard-boiled eggs (see page 75).

WHY: It results in very moist, tender food because very little liquid escapes while cooking; it develops flavors of soups very quickly, and it has a Sauté function so meats can be seared before pressure cooking. It saves time with many recipes!

WHY NOT: There's a bit of a learning curve when you start using it. It takes up countertop space and doesn't make large quantities of food. And it doesn't always save time because of the pressure build and release time.

Food processor

WHAT: A countertop appliance with a blade inside a bowl. Generally used for pureeing, blending, pulverizing, slicing, and grating.

WHEN: For turning cookies into crumbs, blitzing sauces, blending salad dressing, grating bulk cheese, and quickly slicing veggies. It can take care of most functions a blender would handle.

WHY: It speeds up food prep and processes ingredients more thoroughly than doing it by hand.

WHY NOT: There are several blade attachments to keep track of and a few little parts to clean.

Stand mixer

WHAT: A countertop appliance designed for mixing, beating, and whipping.

WHEN: For making batters, frostings, doughs, and whipped cream. Alternate uses include mashing potatoes and shredding cooked chicken.

WHY: A powerful motor makes beating and whipping a pleasure, not a chore.

WHY NOT: It takes up countertop space and can be hard to move around, and it can have multiple attachments that are hard to store and keep track of.

Instant Pot 101

Some recipes in this book use an Instant Pot! While I also include standard cooking instructions for all those recipes, I want to share a few basics with you in case, like me, you're a latecomer to the Instant Pot world. When I first received one from my friend Hyacinth as a birthday gift, I was intimidated because, quite frankly, there were a heck of a lot of buttons. But I quickly learned the ropes. I hope this little primer helps you do the same!

Note: This is not an exhaustive manual on how to use every feature of your Instant Pot. Please consult your owner's instruction booklet for important details!

WHAT THE HECK IS IT?

An Instant Pot is an electronic appliance that has a pressure cooker function, a sauté function, and a slow cooker function and can handle other specific tasks, such as making yogurt. I use only my Instant Pot's **PRESSURE** and **SAUTÉ** functions (usually within the same recipe; see pages 177 and 199), so that's what I'll cover in this primer. (Again, consult your Instant Pot booklet to learn about all it can do!)

WHAT IS PRESSURE COOKING?

Pressure cooking is an age-old cooking method that involves sealing food inside a pot (always with some form of liquid) and heating it for a period of time without letting any steam escape. Because the steam stays inside the vessel, the temperature can climb much higher than the regular boiling point of 212°F; it can get as high as 250°F. Because of both the high heat and the fact that all moisture stays inside, food cooks more quickly and retains a level of moisture that wouldn't be possible in standard pots and pans. My grandma Helen always had a traditional (non-electronic!) pressure cooker on her stovetop and used it all the time.

HOW DOES THE SAUTÉ FUNCTION COME INTO PLAY?

The beauty of the Sauté function is that when you're getting ready to pressure cook a roast or stew, you can first brown or sear the meat right inside the Instant Pot, then add the liquid, seasoning, herbs, and other ingredients before putting on the lid and starting the pressure-cooking process. With slow cookers, on the other hand, it's always necessary to brown and sear in a separate pot before transferring everything over, so being able to do it in the same pot is incredibly handy.

WHAT HAPPENS TO ALL THE PRESSURE AND STEAM ONCE THE FOOD STOPS COOKING?

First, it's important to note that both the time it takes for the pressure to build and the machine to

2. YOU CAN MANUALLY RELEASE THE STEAM YOURSELF BY SWITCHING THE VALVE TO "VENTING." (THIS IS CALLED "QUICK RELEASE.")

I always use the handle of a wooden spoon to open the valve, because the steam that blasts out of the valve is obviously very hot! But it releases it quickly, usually within a minute. It's best to use this method when the liquid inside the pot is water or clear broth without a lot of food particles, as when cooking hard-boiled eggs and simple soups. With pot roasts, stews, and chunky soups, quick release can send small particles in the steam and clog the pressure valve.

3. YOU CAN DO A COMBINATION OF THE TWO, WHICH IS WHAT I ALMOST ALWAYS PREFER.

I let the machine release pressure naturally for anywhere from 10 to 20 minutes, then I push open the valve to release the rest quickly. Best of both worlds!

HOW DOES THE TYPICAL RECIPE PLAY OUT?

There are lots of different recipes for the Instant Pot, but here's how mine (again, usually pot roasts, stews, and soups) typically go:

1. I plug in the machine. Turns out this is important! (Ha ha.)

2. I push the Sauté button to start heating it up. (If you aren't browning meat or sautéeing vegetables first, skip this and go to step 5.)

3. When the bottom of the metal insert is hot, I add oil just as I would if I were using a Dutch oven on the stove.

4. I brown the meat on all sides, using tongs to move it around.

5. Next, I pour in stock or wine, then add herbs, vegetables, or whatever else my recipe calls for. Again, at this point the Instant Pot is no different from a regular pot on a stove.

6. Here's where things change: I attach the lid (it beeps to let you know it is properly attached), then make sure the valve on top of the lid is lined up with the word "Sealing." This will ensure that the pressure cooker will seal and stop releasing steam

seal and the time it takes for the pressure to release after cooking are not included in the official cooking time of a recipe. So, for example, if a recipe calls for you to cook a roast for 50 minutes, you input "50 minutes." But it might take 15 minutes for the pressure to build up before the 50-minute clock begins and 20 minutes for the pressure to release after cooking ends—so you'd actually be looking at 85 minutes total.

After the cooking time has elapsed, you have three choices for releasing the steam:

1. YOU CAN ALLOW THE MACHINE TO AUTOMATICALLY RELEASE THE STEAM. (THIS IS CALLED "NATURAL RELEASE".)

This takes away the guesswork on your part and is ideal if you have the time to wait. The machine very slowly lets small amounts of pressure/steam release over a period of time. As a safety mechanism, it won't let you open the lid until a sufficient amount of pressure has released. Sometimes this extra pressure-release time actually helps the food to continue cooking a little more slowly and results in a better dish.

once the temperature rises. If you don't seal the valve, it's no different from a regular pot on the stove because steam will release the whole time it's cooking.

7. Next, I push one of the pressure cooker control buttons. Manual is the one I use the most, and that just means I'm going to tell the Instant Pot how long to pressure cook what's inside rather than use one of the preprogrammed buttons. I usually cook things anywhere from 20 minutes to 90 minutes. Most recipes will tell you how long!

8. Over a period of 10 to 20 minutes, I'll hear the Instant Pot working more and more as the temperature rises. During this time, some steam will be released, but that's normal. It's just building up heat until it gets hot enough to seal. Once it seals, a little float valve pops up and you know the machine is doing its thing.

9. After the cooking time is up, I don't do anything yet. I give it 10 to 20 minutes to naturally release pressure/steam. (The timer will actually count backward, so you'll be able to see how many minutes have expired since the cooking time ended!)

10. When some of the pressure has been naturally released, I use a wooden spoon to open the valve and quick release the rest. You'll know it's ready when the steam stops coming out and the float valve pops back down!

11. I open the lid and serve up the food! Yum.

I'm not a big fancy-gadget person when it comes to cooking, but I've really learned to enjoy the Instant Pot possibilities!

I hope this little how-to will take the pressure off (get it?) and encourage you to try it.

Labels in This Book

I tried to slap at least one label on each of the recipes in the book, just to give you more context for when to whip them up.

Lower-carb. Not to be confused with *low carb* in the strict Atkins or Keto diet sense, these recipes are simply a little lighter than the regular version, with a little less flour and sugar.

Make-ahead. Recipes with the Make-ahead label lend themselves to being made ahead of time and kept in the fridge or freezer. These'll save your sanity.

Quick and Easy. Speaking of saving your sanity . . . we all need a good batch of quick-to-prep-and-cook dishes, and this list will make you a happier, more peaceful person. Promise!

Freezes Well. I love to stock my freezer with dinners and desserts, but sometimes it's hard to know which ones freeze well. I take out the guesswork for you with these recipes.

Family-friendly. Whether you've got a houseful of kiddos and/or a picky life partner (ahem), these crowd-pleasing dishes are sure to get the thumbs-up from everyone.

Great for Guests. Whether you're having your boss over for dinner or just a casual group of friends, these are the recipes that are particularly suited for company. You'll wow them!

Indulgent. Over-the-top, decadent, ridiculous recipes, with no regard for calories, carb counts, or anything else that's logical and sensible. (Psst. Smaller portions are the key!)

Ladd on his horse at dawn. His favorite place.

Breakfast

Are you an I've-gotta-have-protein-in-the-morning person? Or a gimme-all-the-carbs-with-my-coffee person? Or does that change from day to day? Here are some new breakfast dishes for your arsenal, from simple scrambles to creative casseroles—and some portable options for those times you and your family have to dine while you dash. Good morning!

TODD'S GRIDDLE SANDWICHES

MAKES 12 SANDWICHES

WHAT: A homemade version of the Mickey D's classic.

WHEN: Breakfast on the go! (Breakfast at the table is fine, too.)

WHY: Because it's a McGriddle, man! Too crazy not to love. Because it's not actually a McGriddle.

I have a confession to make, and it isn't an easy one to admit. It isn't that I occasionally go through the drive-thru of McDonald's with my boys. It's that *I actually feel funny and uneasy* going through the drive-thru of McDonald's with my boys. See, I write cookbooks. I also have a cooking show on TV. In both settings, I extol the fun and enjoyment of making home-cooked meals for my family, which, of course, is always my preference. So for whatever reason, during those times when I'm sitting in the drive-thru after ordering, I sometimes feel like a siren is going to go off and a big spotlight is going to shine down from the sky and into the driver's seat of my (caked with mud, but that's a different confession) pickup, and I will have to explain to some unknown entity why I am sitting in the drive-thru of McDonald's when I write books and film TV shows about the virtues of home cooking. But then I come to my senses, remind myself that I've gotta keep it real, and pay for the boys' big bag of food (which almost always includes a McGriddle for Todd, because they are now on McDonald's all-day menu and they are also Todd's favorite food on earth).

Then I peel out as fast as I can and speed away before someone sees me.

Cooking spray

18 large eggs

4 cups (1 quart) whole milk, plus more if needed for thinning

1½ teaspoons kosher salt

1 teaspoon black pepper

6 slices thick-cut bacon

6 sausage patties

3 cups plus 2 tablespoons all-purpose flour

2 tablespoons baking powder

1 tablespoon sugar

2 teaspoons vanilla extract

4 tablespoons (½ stick) salted butter, plus more for frying

12 slices American cheese

MAPLE BUTTER

8 tablespoons (1 stick) salted butter, softened

2 tablespoons maple syrup

1. Preheat the oven to 350°F. Line a sheet pan with parchment paper and coat the paper with cooking spray.

2. In a large bowl, whisk 16 of the eggs, 1 cup of the milk, 1 teaspoon of the salt, and the pepper.

3. Pour it into the sheet pan . . .

4. And bake until the eggs are completely set, 15 to 17 minutes.

8. In a separate bowl, whisk the remaining 3 cups milk, remaining 2 eggs, and the vanilla.

12. Fry the pancakes on both sides until golden, about 2 minutes per side. Set aside and keep warm.

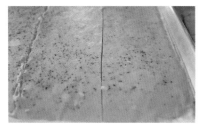

5. Slice the eggs into 12 squares. After 5 minutes, peel the egg squares off the parchment. Set aside.

9. Stir the milk mixture into the flour mixture until halfway combined. Melt the 4 tablespoons butter and add it to the bowl.

13. Make the maple butter: In a medium bowl, combine the butter and maple syrup . . .

6. In a skillet, fry the bacon and sausage until done. Remove from the pan and keep warm.

10. Stir gently until incorporated, splashing in more milk if the batter is too thick.

14. And stir to combine with a rubber spatula.

7. In a large bowl, whisk together the flour, baking powder, sugar, and remaining ½ teaspoon salt.

11. Melt some butter on a griddle over medium-low heat. In batches, drop 2 tablespoons batter onto the griddle for each pancake.

15. To assemble, spread maple butter on each pancake.

16. Top 6 of the pancakes with cheese, a folded-over square of egg, and a sausage patty.

17. Top another 6 pancakes the same way, except with bacon instead of sausage.

Yum yum! They're the secret to Todd's happiness! And I didn't have to go through the drive-thru to get 'em.

18. Pop on the lids, butter side down, and serve immediately. Or freeze, wrapped in individual squares of foil. To reheat, just heat the foil-wrapped sandwich in a 350°F oven for 25 minutes.

Variations

» *Use all sausage or all bacon—whatever your family prefers!*

» *Switch up the cheese with pepper Jack or another favorite.*

Todd's a sweetie. I think I'll keep him.

BLISTERED TOMATO AND EGG WHITE SCRAMBLE

MAKES 4 TO 6 SERVINGS

WHAT: Scrambled egg whites with creamy goat cheese and juicy blistered tomatoes.

WHEN: Any time you have a hankering for a fresh, healthy (and pretty!) breakfast or brunch.

WHY: Because the light texture of the whites is the perfect pairing for creamy goat cheese. The blistered tomatoes are a complete treasure!

Sometimes I love a good egg white scramble, not because I have anything against egg yolks (on the contrary, I'm going to mandate that at least one mention of egg yolks winds up somewhere in my epitaph), but because I find scrambled egg whites to be a completely different dish from regular scrambled eggs, and it's fun to have the change. They take on an almost tofu-type texture (which, because I love tofu, I consider a good thing!), and they lend themselves so perfectly to other yummy ingredients (hint hint: tomatoes and basil!). The whites in this particular scramble are whisked with goat cheese before cooking, too, which ushers in a whole new degree of awesome. You'll love this breakfast!

12 egg whites

4 ounces goat cheese, plus more for serving

½ teaspoon kosher salt

½ teaspoon black pepper, plus more to taste

2 tablespoons olive oil

1 cup grape tomatoes

12 basil leaves, cut into chiffonade

1. Crack the eggs and separate the whites into a large bowl and whisk until well combined.

2. Break up the goat cheese into chunks and add it to the whites.

3. Vigorously whisk to incorporate the goat cheese into the egg whites. There will be little bits of goat cheese visible.

4. Add the salt and pepper and whisk. Set aside.

7. Remove the tomatoes to a plate.

10. Continue cooking and stirring until the whites are fully cooked, 5 to 7 minutes.

5. Heat a nonstick skillet over medium-high heat and add 1 tablespoon of the olive oil. The oil should be just about smoking. Add the tomatoes . . .

8. Return the skillet to the stove and reduce the heat to medium-low. Add the remaining 1 tablespoon oil to the pan, then pour in the egg white mixture.

11. Stir in the tomatoes, along with any juices that have collected on the plate.

6. And toss them around the pan for about a minute, until they have blackened bits.

9. Use a heatproof silicone spatula to scrape around the edges and stir gently to keep the whites from browning.

12. Serve the eggs with a few goat cheese crumbles and basil on top.

BROWN BUTTER GRANOLA CLUSTERS

MAKES ABOUT 10 CUPS

WHAT: Deep (and I do mean deep) golden brown crunchy clusters of yummy granola.

WHEN: Breakfast time, after school, sports practice, car nibbles, movie munching. (Just avoid the library if you can help it.)

WHY: The brown butter sends this already scrumptious granola completely over the top. And the grains and nuts are good for ya.

Any butter contained in any granola recipe is, by its nature, "brown," since granola is baked in the oven, thereby browning the butter. (I think I'll say "butter" a few more times.) But if you start with the butter already browned before the granola bakes, you wind up with the deepest deep-golden granola you can possibly achieve. And the flavor. *The flavor!* Try it and you'll get it. Promise.

1 cup (2 sticks) salted butter

6 cups old-fashioned rolled oats

¼ cup vegetable oil

1 teaspoon kosher salt

1 cup packed brown sugar

½ cup honey

¼ cup molasses

1 tablespoon vanilla extract

1 cup crispy rice cereal, such as Rice Krispies

1 cup wheat germ

½ cup dried cranberries

½ cup finely chopped pecans

½ cup hulled pumpkin seeds

¼ cup roughly chopped almonds

¼ cup flaxseeds

Coconut oil spray

1. To brown the butter, place 1½ sticks of the butter in a medium skillet over medium heat.

2. Cook, swirling the skillet to keep the butter moving around, until it melts and bubbles up, 3 to 4 minutes.

3. When a foam forms on top and the butter is a medium golden brown, remove the skillet from the heat (it will continue browning in the skillet over the next 30 seconds or so!).

4. Pour the butter and any solids into a bowl and let it cool completely, about 30 minutes.

5. Preheat the oven to 350°F.

6. Melt the remaining ½ stick butter in the microwave. In a bowl, combine the oats, oil, melted butter (not the brown butter), and salt.

7. Toss until the oats are all coated.

8. Spread the mixture on two sheet pans and bake until toasted, about 12 minutes, carefully shaking the pans twice.

9. Set aside to cool a bit. Reduce the oven temperature to 325°F.

10. In a medium saucepan, combine the brown sugar, honey, molasses, and vanilla.

11. Stir the mixture until combined, then heat over medium heat, stirring, until just beginning to boil.

12. Remove the pan from the heat, add the brown butter to the pan, and stir.

It's very sticky, so you'll need to work quickly!

17. Store in a jar until ready to use. (Or you can package it up and give as gifts!)

13. Line the two sheet pans with foil and thoroughly coat with coconut oil spray. In a large bowl, combine the toasted oats, rice cereal, wheat germ, cranberries, pecans, pumpkin seeds, almonds, and flaxseeds.

15. Tip the mixture onto the pans. Spread it out and bake until golden, about 30 minutes.

16. Let the mixture cool and set completely, then use a fork to break it into clusters.

14. Toss to combine, then pour in the butter-molasses mixture, stirring as you pour.

Variations

» *Drizzle the pans of cooled granola with melted semisweet chocolate and let it set completely, then break into clusters.*

» *Cut the granola into bars immediately after the pans are removed from the oven. Let them sit until cool before you remove the bars from the pans.*

» *Make yogurt and fruit parfaits with alternating layers of yogurt, granola, and fruit.*

18. Eat in a bowl with milk (as cereal) or top bowls of yogurt with the clusters.

BREAKFAST PARCELS

MAKES 4 SERVINGS

WHAT: Individually baked foil parcels with sausage, peppers, onions, potatoes, and egg.

WHEN: When you don't want to stand over a stove to make your breakfast. (Let the oven do the cooking!)

WHY: Because pulling the parcels out of the oven and peeling back that foil is like opening a gift from Breakfast Santa.

There's something about foil parcels of cooked food that make my heart go pitter-pat, and you'll see more than one recipe for them in this book. I just love the concept of mixing a big bowl of ingredients together, dividing them among foil sheets, folding them into parcels, and throwing them in the oven. The best part is opening them up and seeing what's inside! And then, of course, eating what's inside. (I'm so predictable.)

3 tablespoons olive oil

2 tablespoons whole-grain mustard

1 tablespoon Montreal steak seasoning

1 teaspoon kosher salt, plus more for sprinkling

2 medium russet potatoes, scrubbed and cut into medium dice

1 red bell pepper, seeded and cut into large dice

1 green bell pepper, seeded and cut into large dice

1 red onion, cut into medium chunks

3 cups stemmed torn kale leaves

14 maple breakfast sausage links (not precooked), halved crosswise

4 large eggs

Black pepper

3 green onions, thinly sliced, for serving

1. Preheat the oven to 450°F. Cut four 10-inch squares of foil.

2. In a small bowl, combine the olive oil, mustard, Montreal seasoning, and salt.

3. In a large bowl, combine the potatoes, bell peppers, and onion.

4. Pour the mustard mixture on top . . .

5. And toss a few times, then toss in the kale.

6. Place one-quarter of the mixture on each foil sheet.

7. Arrange 7 sausage halves on top of each . . .

8. Then wrap the parcels by gathering the two ends, folding them down the middle, and gathering up the ends. Place them on a sheet pan and bake for 20 minutes.

9. Remove the pan from the oven and carefully open each parcel, pressing the foil open. Crack an egg onto the middle of each parcel, sprinkle the eggs with salt and pepper, and return the pan to the oven.

10. Bake for 8 to 10 minutes, until the egg is done to your liking. Sprinkle with green onions and serve!

Variations

» *Use a larger, fully cooked sausage link cut into thick slices instead of the breakfast links.*

» *Use any combination of your favorite vegetables: mushrooms, zucchini, and so forth.*

» *Fry an egg on the stovetop and place it on the finished parcel if you prefer not to bake the egg in the oven.*

BRAINSTORM: FOIL BREAKFAST PARCEL IDEAS!

Follow the same general method for these parcels . . . or use this list as a springboard for your own ideas. Experimentation is tasty fun!

- ✿ Diced ham, asparagus pieces, peeled and diced sweet potatoes, cracked eggs, chopped chives

- ✿ Sliced chicken-apple sausage, yellow bell pepper strips, sliced onion, cracked eggs, parsley

- ✿ Cubed ciabatta, whisked eggs, splash of milk, sugar, cinnamon, cooked bacon bits

- ✿ Torn raisin bread, sliced smoked sausage, apple slices, butter, brown sugar, maple syrup

- ✿ Corn tortilla wedges, diced Spanish chorizo, diced onion, diced bell pepper, sliced jarred jalapeño, cubed pepper Jack cheese, cracked eggs, salsa

- ✿ Canadian bacon slices, red bell pepper chunks, frozen hash browns, whisked eggs, sharp Cheddar, sliced green onions

- ✿ Torn croissants, diced ham, whisked eggs, grated Swiss, sliced green onions

- ✿ Crumbled granola, mini marshmallows, sliced bananas, mini chocolate chips, turbinado sugar

- ✿ Cubed French bread, cream cheese chunks, dehydrated onion, whisked eggs, sharp Cheddar, chopped chives

PEACHY SLOW COOKER OATMEAL

MAKES 8 TO 10 SERVINGS

WHAT: Delicious, peachy oatmeal you can make overnight in your slow cooker.

WHEN: When you want breakfast to be ready right when your feet hit the floor.

WHY: Because this oatmeal is loaded with love—which, of course, is the best kind of oatmeal.

I'm just going to say it: I was never a big fan of oatmeal. That is, of course, until I learned to doctor it (translation: absolutely load it up) with brown sugar, cream, and other good things. And now I totally *love* oatmeal—go figure! I especially love it made overnight in the slow cooker, because you can go to bed and have the sweetest dreams knowing that breakfast will be waiting for you when you wake up. I'm a big fan of oatmeal. Have I ever mentioned that?

2 cups steel-cut oats

4 cups frozen peach slices

⅔ cup packed brown sugar

1 tablespoon vanilla extract

1 teaspoon kosher salt

1 cup coconut flakes

1 cup sliced almonds

2 cups golden raisins

1 cup whole milk

¼ cup heavy cream, plus more for serving

1 cup fresh blueberries, for serving

Honey, for serving

1. Pour the oats into the slow cooker . . .

3. The brown sugar . . .

5. The salt . . .

2. Then top with the frozen peaches . . .

4. The vanilla . . .

6. And 8 cups (2 quarts) water.

7. Give the mixture a gentle stir, then place the lid on and cook on low for 8 hours (or overnight).

11. Guess what? We have been in a time warp and the oatmeal is done. Look at how dark and delicious it is.

15. Stir and keep warm until serving.

8. Meanwhile, prepare the toppings: In a dry skillet, toast the coconut flakes over medium heat, shaking the pan frequently to toast.

12. Stir the oatmeal well, gently scraping the bottom of the insert to make sure all the caramelized bits have been loosened.

16. Serve in a bowl with blueberries, the toasted coconut and almonds, a drizzle of honey, and a little more cream.

9. When golden brown, let it cool and store it in an airtight container.

13. The next step is to add the golden raisins . . .

Bryce isn't a little boy anymore! (Sniff sniff.)

10. Do the same with the sliced almonds!

14. Along with the milk and cream.

SLOW COOKER BROCCOLI EGG CASSEROLE

MAKES 6 TO 8 SERVINGS

WHAT: A veggie-forward breakfast casserole made in your slow cooker.

WHEN: A lazy weekend breakfast or brunch.

WHY: Because sometimes you're in the mood for a meatless morning meal.

I've mentioned before that when I was growing up, ours was not a slow cooker household. It wasn't that my mom took any particular stance against slow cookers; it's just that the contraption wasn't part of her cooking routine. As such, I raised my own kids for years without benefiting from the life-saving ease of slow cooker dishes, and now that I've awakened that part of my soul, I feel I need a therapy session with my mother to explore the ways she shortchanged me by not teaching me the slow cooker way of life. (Just kidding, Mom—you more than made up for it with that lasagna of yours . . .)

Here's a lovely, simple slow cooker casserole that'll make your mornings a happier time. If you get up before daylight, you can have breakfast ready by nine. Or you can call it a lazy weekend brunch if that's more your speed. Mom, I'll make it for ya next time you visit! Right after our therapy session, of course . . .

Cooking spray

1 head broccoli, cut into small florets (3½ to 4 cups)

1 red bell pepper, seeded and cut into medium dice

1½ cups grated Cheddar cheese

3 green onions, thinly sliced

12 large eggs

1 cup half-and-half

½ teaspoon kosher salt

¼ teaspoon black pepper

1. Generously coat the inside of a 6-quart slow cooker with cooking spray.

2. Add half the broccoli . . .

3. Half the bell pepper . . .

4. And half the Cheddar and green onions . . .

8. Pour the egg mixture over the top.

SWAP-INS

Add or substitute any of the following. Play with different combinations to make your own!

- ❀ Frozen diced hash browns
- ❀ Cooked crumbled breakfast sausage
- ❀ Cooked crumbled bacon
- ❀ Baby spinach
- ❀ Grated Swiss cheese
- ❀ Sautéed mushrooms
- ❀ Jarred pesto
- ❀ Sun-dried tomatoes
- ❀ Quartered artichoke hearts
- ❀ A mix of chopped fresh herbs

5. Then repeat the layers once more.

9. Then cover and cook on low for 3½ to 4 hours . . .

STANDARD OVEN DIRECTIONS

Preheat the oven to 350°F.

Follow the instructions here, except layer the ingredients in a buttered 9 x 13-inch baking dish. Cover the dish with foil and bake for 25 minutes. Remove the foil and continue to bake until the cheese is browned and bubbling and the casserole is cooked through, another 20 minutes. Cut into squares and serve.

6. In a large pitcher or bowl, combine the eggs, half-and-half, salt, and pepper . . .

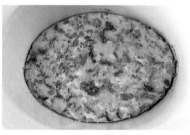

10. Until golden around the edges and just barely set in the center. The mixture of textures is nice!

7. And whisk until light and fluffy, about 1 minute.

11. Serve it up by the (generous) spoonful!

BERRY BREAKFAST TARTS

MAKES 8 TARTS

WHAT: A make-at-home version of the breakfast pastries we all loved as kids.

WHEN: Portable breakfast on busy mornings, or after-school snack.

WHY: The possibilities for fillings and glazes are endless! You'll be hooked.

Those store-bought breakfast pastries that shall remain nameless (Pop-Tarts) are in the category of grocery items I flat-out refuse to buy anymore—not because I cherish my family too much to fill their bodies with such things (I do cherish them, just not in that way), but because once my boys hit the age of thirteen, I learned the hard way that boxes of those store-bought breakfast pastries that shall remain nameless (Pop-Tarts) completely disappear before the sun sets on whichever day I purchase them. And it doesn't matter if I were to buy a regular box or a value-size box. *Gone.* It's as if it's against a teenage boy's religion to allow a box of the things to make it past sunset.

These homemade babies are a great compromise—although if you do have teenage boys, you may have to hide them here or there around the kitchen. I suggest inside pots with lids, on top of the fridge, wrapped tightly inside the air-conditioning vent . . . you get the idea.

3 cups all-purpose flour

2 tablespoons sugar

¼ teaspoon kosher salt

1 cup (2 sticks) cold salted butter, cut into small cubes

2 large eggs

1 tablespoon white vinegar

5 to 8 tablespoons ice water

1 cup plus 2 tablespoons mixed berry jam

1¼ cups powdered sugar, sifted

2 tablespoons whole milk

4 drops neon purple food coloring

Rainbow sprinkles

1. In a large bowl, whisk together the flour, sugar, and salt.

2. Add the butter . . .

3. And, using a pastry cutter, work the butter into the flour mixture until it resembles coarse crumbs.

4. Lightly beat one of the eggs and add to the mixture . . .

5. Then add the vinegar and 5 tablespoons ice water.

6. Stir until the dough just comes together, adding up to 3 more tablespoons ice water if the mixture is too crumbly.

7. Form the dough into a disc and wrap tightly in plastic wrap. Chill for 1 hour.

8. Preheat the oven to 400°F. Divide the dough in half and roll one portion into a large rectangle, about 12 x 16 inches. (The dough should be rolled very thin.)

9. Using a pizza cutter or knife, cut off the rough edges, then cut into eight equal-size rectangles.

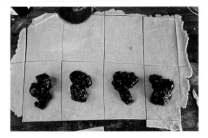

10. Place about 1½ tablespoons of the jam into the center of four of the rectangles.

11. Whisk the remaining egg with 1 tablespoon water and brush it around the edges of the four rectangles.

12. Place the remaining rectangles over the jam, pressing the edges together and gently forcing out any large air pockets . . .

13. Then crimp the edges with a fork to seal. Repeat with the other portion of dough.

14. Place them on two parchment-lined sheet pans and pierce them with a fork to vent.

15. Bake until golden and slightly crisp around the edges, 16 to 18 minutes. Let cool completely.

16. In a bowl, whisk together the powdered sugar, milk, remaining jam, and food coloring to make the glaze.

17. Spoon the glaze over the pastries . . .

18. Then add the sprinkles! Let the glaze set completely, then pack them in airtight containers and hide them inside the air-conditioning vent.

These are totally my jam!

Variations

» *Change the jam flavor to whatever variety you'd like!*

» *Omit the food coloring for a more natural glaze color.*

» *Add lemon curd, Marshmallow Fluff, Nutella, or any fillings you'd like!*

» *Top with ganache for more of a chocolaty treat.*

TEX-MEX SHEET PAN BREAKFAST

MAKES 6 TO 8 SERVINGS

WHAT: An abundant one-pan breakfast with eggs, sausage, tortillas, and fixins!

WHEN: When you need breakfast for a crowd!

WHY: Because Tex-Mex eggs are the best eggs.

I've reached a point in my journey in which I am no longer able to eat eggs without some form of hot sauce. I remember years ago, I would poke fun at the cowboys who carried bottles of Tabasco and Cholula in the glove compartments of their pickups "in case of emergencies." As happens with most everything I've ever poked fun at in my life, I now do the same thing. This sheet pan breakfast takes the whole eggs-with-hot-sauce concept to a new level, and is so easy to throw together for a crowd. Change it up with different varieties of veggies, sausage, and cheese if you'd like. The choices are yours!

One 28-ounce bag frozen diced hash browns

1 small red onion, cut into ½-inch dice

½ jalapeño, sliced into rounds

3 tablespoons salted butter, melted

3 tablespoons olive oil

½ teaspoon kosher salt, plus more for sprinkling

½ teaspoon black pepper, plus more for sprinkling

4 corn tortillas

4 ounces Mexican chorizo

8 large eggs

½ cup grated pepper Jack cheese

2 avocados, cut into ½-inch dice

⅓ cup pico de gallo (see page 107)

Hot sauce

Sour cream, for serving

Cilantro leaves, for serving

1. Preheat the oven to 425°F.

2. Combine the hash browns, onion, and jalapeño on a sheet pan.

3. Drizzle the melted butter and olive oil on top, then season with the salt and pepper and toss to coat.

4. Bake for 25 minutes, tossing halfway through. Remove the pan from the oven and reduce the temperature to 375°F.

5. Stack the tortillas and cut into 6 wedges.

6. Tuck the tortilla wedges into the potatoes . . .

7. Then open the package of chorizo . . .

8. And use a fork to drop bite-size pieces onto the pan. Keep them small, as they need to fully cook in the oven by the time the rest of the ingredients are cooked.

9. Space the chorizo evenly over the pan.

10. Crack the eggs over the top (don't worry if you break a yolk or two!), then sprinkle with salt and pepper.

11. Return the sheet pan to the oven and bake until the eggs are cooked to your liking and the chorizo is cooked, 12 to 15 minutes. The chorizo should be hot and sizzling.

12. Sprinkle on the Jack . . .

13. The avocados . . .

14. The pico de gallo . . .

15. And the hot sauce to taste.

16. Use a spatula to cut large squares of the breakfast . . .

17. And serve with sour cream, cilantro leaves, and more hot sauce!

BRAINSTORM: SHEET PAN BREAKFAST IDEAS

Experiment with different forms of potatoes, veggies, proteins, and eggs. Try to make little nests with potatoes and veggies on which to crack the eggs. Here are some inspirations!

❀ Beaten eggs, baby spinach, diced red onion, grated Swiss, halved cherry tomatoes, pesto (frittata style!)

❀ Leftover French bread torn into chunks, diced ham, asparagus pieces, frozen diced hash browns, grated pepper Jack cheese, diced onion, cracked eggs

❀ Chicken-apple sausage links, peeled and diced sweet potatoes, diced onion, diced red and yellow bell pepper, fajita seasoning

❀ Frozen shredded hash browns, Canadian bacon slices, Provolone slices, red onion slices, yellow bell pepper rings, zucchini slices, diced tomato

❀ Halved Brussels sprouts, bacon pieces, halved button mushrooms, sliced red onion, cracked eggs

❀ Buttered and halved Texas toast, pork sausage links, peeled and diced sweet potatoes, diced onion, cracked eggs, minced parsley

❀ Frozen crinkle-cut French fries, bacon bits, chopped red and green bell pepper, sharp Cheddar, cracked eggs, hot sauce

GIANT CINNAMON ROLL

MAKES 12 SERVINGS

WHAT: A gargantuan cinnamon roll baked in a skillet!

WHEN: Any time you want to wow the cinnamon roll lovers in your life.

WHY: Because it bakes up like a coffee cake and looks incredible and inviting.

My cinnamon rolls, which were originally my mom's cinnamon rolls, are legendary, and I don't say that in a pat-myself-on-the-back way. It's just that the cinnamon rolls my mom taught me how to make truly are the best cinnamon rolls I've ever tasted, and the best cinnamon rolls *you've* ever tasted—even if you haven't tasted them yet. After seeing the gigantic cinnamon roll trend on the Internet, I decided to give it a try using my mom's recipe. The results were astounding! And very, very, very large!

Come to mama!

DOUGH

2 cups whole milk

½ cup vegetable oil

½ cup granulated sugar

1 package (2¼ teaspoons) active dry yeast

4½ cups all-purpose flour, plus more for dusting

½ teaspoon baking powder

¼ teaspoon baking soda

1½ teaspoons salt

FILLING

1½ cups (3 sticks) salted butter, melted

¾ cup granulated sugar

2 teaspoons ground cinnamon

MAPLE ICING

1 pound powdered sugar, sifted

¼ cup whole milk, plus more as needed

¼ cup strong brewed coffee

1½ teaspoons maple extract

3 tablespoons salted butter, melted

1. Butter a 10- to 12-inch ovenproof skillet. Set it aside.

2. Make the dough: In a medium saucepan, combine the milk, oil, and sugar and set over medium heat.

4. Sprinkle the yeast over the mixture and let it sit for 1 minute.

6. Stir until just combined (it will be very sticky), then cover the pot with a clean kitchen towel. Set the dough aside in a draft-free place for 1 hour.

3. Heat until bubbles start to form on the sides of the pan, then turn off the heat. Set the mixture aside to cool to a little warmer than lukewarm.

5. Add 4 cups of the flour.

7. Remove the towel (the mixture should have doubled in size; if not, allow it to rise a while longer) and add the baking powder, baking soda, salt, and the remaining ½ cup flour.

8. Stir thoroughly to combine. You can cover and chill the dough at this point, or you can continue with the cinnamon roll!

9. On a floured surface, roll out the dough into a large rectangle, about 25 x 10 inches.

10. Prepare the filling: Pour the melted butter over the rolled dough and use a brush to spread it all over the surface.

11. In a small bowl, stir together the sugar and cinnamon . . .

12. And sprinkle the cinnamon sugar all over the buttered surface.

13. Use a pizza cutter or knife to cut the dough into 4 long, even strips.

14. Starting at one end, roll up one of the strips, keeping the cut edge as lined up as possible.

15. When it's rolled up, place it on the end of the next strip and keep rolling, lining up the cut ends as much as possible. Continue rolling with the other strips. You'll have one really scary, huge roll of dough!

16. Carefully pick up the roll and place it in the center of the skillet, neat edges up. Cover it with a kitchen towel and place in a warm spot for 45 minutes to rise.

17. Preheat the oven to 350°F. When the rising time has ended, place the pan in the oven and bake for 25 minutes . . .

18. Then cover it lightly with foil to avoid overbrowning. Bake until done in the center, 20 to 25 minutes more.

20. Meanwhile, make the icing: In a large bowl, combine the powdered sugar, milk, coffee, maple extract, and melted butter.

22. When the baking time is up (don't be concerned if it kinda goes catawampus in the oven—that just means you're cool), remove the skillet from the oven . . .

24. Slice it into wedges and serve!

21. Whisk until smooth, splashing in more milk if needed for thinning.

23. And pour the icing all over the top, around the edges, and in the center. Let sit for 10 to 15 minutes to allow the icing to ooze down into the cracks and crevices.

Helpful hint

You can make the dough the night before and store it, covered, in the fridge. Then just make the cinnamon roll the next morning!

Father and son. And football!

GREEN EGGS AND HAM SCRAMBLE

MAKES 4 TO 6 SERVINGS

WHAT: Pesto scrambled eggs with spinach and diced ham.

WHEN: Any bright, sunny morning of the week! (Or any dark, cloudy morning.)

WHY: The amount of spinach in each serving would make Popeye proud!

When I used to read the Dr. Seuss classic as a child, I always tried to imagine what green eggs and ham would taste like. Oh, I saw what they *looked* like in the book's illustrations, and they sure weren't pretty: white eggs with bright green centers (ew), and a big ol' chunk of equally bright green ham (ew again), with a big carving fork sticking out of the side. I loved the book and its charming cadence, but wanted no part of the breakfast feast Sam-I-Am was attempting to foist on . . . wait. Who was the central character in *Green Eggs and Ham*? To the best of my recollection, I'm thinking he was nameless. I've never realized that until now, and I'm old enough to be a millennial's mother. It's a good thing I didn't wait a millennium to make my own version of green eggs and ham, though, because I love it!

8 large eggs

2 tablespoons prepared pesto, store-bought or homemade (see page 161)

½ teaspoon kosher salt

1 teaspoon black pepper

½ cup whole milk

2 tablespoons salted butter

One 1-pound ham steak, cut into small cubes

3 cups baby spinach

½ cup freshly grated white Cheddar cheese

1 tablespoon minced fresh chives

1. Place the eggs in a large bowl. Add the pesto, salt, and pepper . . .

3. Add the milk . . .

5. Heat a large nonstick skillet over medium heat. Add the butter and let it melt, then add the ham. Stir and cook for about 3 minutes to fully heat the ham through.

2. And whisk until combined.

4. And whisk again.

6. Add 2 cups of the spinach and stir it in with the ham . . .

7. Then pour in the eggs.

8. Let them sit in the pan without stirring for about a minute . . .

9. Then use a heatproof silicone spatula to begin stirring gently, scraping the pan as you go so that the eggs cook evenly.

10. Continue cooking, stirring and scraping constantly, until the eggs are almost fully set, about 3 minutes.

11. Add the rest of the spinach and the Cheddar . . .

12. And stir until the eggs are fully set, the spinach is wilted, and the cheese is melted.

13. Serve with a sprinkle of chives on top.

SCRAMBLE *THIS*!

There's nothing you can't add to scrambled eggs.

- Diced zucchini
- Pesto
- Grated Parmesan
- Chopped prosciutto
- Diced hash browns
- Chopped smoked salmon
- Torn kale
- Baby spinach
- Diced avocado
- Torn corn tortillas
- Jarred salsa
- Pico de gallo
- Diced bell pepper
- Ketchup (yum!)
- Crumbled feta
- Green olives (trust me!)
- Diced tomato
- Crumbled cooked bacon
- Crumbled cooked sausage
- Crumbled cooked chorizo
- Sliced green onions
- Everything bagel spice

I like green eggs and ham!

INSTANT POT PUMPKIN SPICE OATMEAL

MAKES 6 TO 8 SERVINGS

WHAT: Creamy, comforting steel-cut oats with the flavors of pumpkin spice.

WHEN: Breakfast or afternoon snack.

WHY: Because oatmeal in an Instant Pot is the secret to happiness!

This is one of those "breakfast" dishes that could easily pass as dessert, and that is not an unusual thing for me. These are wonderfully textured (and very creamy) Irish oats, served up just like a pumpkin spice latte at one of those coffee places that dot the landscape of our great country. The toppings are delicious, and while using the Instant Pot is not a huge timesaver, it's wonderful just to throw in the oats and walk away. No stirring! No babysitting! It's a beautiful thing. (And so is this breakfast dish.)

2 cups steel-cut oats

4 cinnamon sticks

Pinch of kosher salt

1 cup packed brown sugar

2 teaspoons pumpkin pie spice, plus more for sprinkling

1 teaspoon vanilla extract

1½ cups heavy cream

Hulled pumpkin seeds, for serving

Jarred caramel sauce, for serving (or see Caramel Apple Quesadillas, page 331)

1. Pour the oats into the Instant Pot.

2. Add 6 cups water, the cinnamon sticks, and the salt, but do not stir. Secure the lid on the Instant Pot and set the pressure valve to Sealing. Cook on Manual for 3 minutes. (Note that it will take a few minutes for the pressure to build before the 3-minute timer begins its countdown.)

3. When the time is up, allow the pressure to release naturally for 15 minutes, then use the handle of a wooden spoon to move the valve to Venting and let the rest of the pressure release. Remove the lid.

4. Use tongs to remove the cinnamon sticks.

5. Add the brown sugar . . .

6. The pumpkin pie spice and vanilla . . .

7. And 1 cup of the cream.

8. Stir everything together. It'll stay warm in the Instant Pot!

9. In a small saucepan, warm the remaining ½ cup cream over medium heat until hot but not boiling.

10. Froth the cream using a milk frothing whisk or a regular whisk. You just want it to be light, like what you'd get in a pumpkin spice latte!

11. To serve, place the cooked oats in a bowl . . .

12. Spoon the frothed cream on top . . .

13. Add the pumpkin seeds and a drizzle of caramel sauce . . .

14. And finally, give it a sprinkling of pumpkin pie spice.

Absolutely delicious!

Variation

» *Add 1 teaspoon instant espresso granules to the Instant Pot before cooking the oats.*

STANDARD COOKING DIRECTIONS

In a medium saucepan, combine the oats, cinnamon sticks, salt, and 6 cups water and bring to a gentle boil over medium heat. Reduce the heat to medium-low and cook, stirring frequently, for 25 minutes. Add the brown sugar, pumpkin pie spice, vanilla, and 1 cup of the heavy cream, then reduce the heat to low and cook for another 10 minutes, or until the oats are to your desired tenderness. Proceed with serving as above.

INSTANT POT EGG BITES

MAKES 7 CHORIZO BITES OR 7 VEGGIE BITES

WHAT: Delicious (and generous) egg bites made in a pressure cooker.

WHEN: When you need a quick protein-rich breakfast on your way out the door.

WHY: Because Starbucks has nothing on these! (No offense, SB!)

I'm a huge fan of Starbucks' egg bites. They're big and satisfying, protein-rich, and low in carbs. Make-at-home egg bites have swept the Instant Pot universe for good reason. They're easy and incredible!

CHORIZO VERSION

8 ounces Mexican chorizo

½ yellow onion, diced

4 large eggs

¼ cup heavy cream

¼ cup sour cream

¼ teaspoon kosher salt

¼ teaspoon black pepper

Cooking spray

⅓ cup grated Monterey Jack cheese

VEGGIE VERSION

2 tablespoons olive oil

¼ cup chopped mushrooms

¼ cup chopped broccoli florets

¼ cup chopped red bell pepper

Kosher salt and black pepper

Cooking spray

4 large eggs

¼ cup heavy cream

¼ cup sour cream

⅓ cup grated sharp Cheddar cheese

1. For the chorizo version: Heat a large skillet over medium heat. Add the chorizo and onion . . .

2. And cook, stirring often, until the onion is soft and the chorizo is fully cooked, 5 to 6 minutes.

3. Transfer to paper towels to drain the excess grease. Set aside to cool.

4. In a large bowl, combine the eggs, heavy cream, sour cream, salt, and pepper.

5. Whisk until light and fluffy, about 1 minute.

6. Generously coat the cups of a silicone egg bite mold (you can find them online!) with cooking spray, then divide the Jack among the cups.

7. Divide the chorizo and onion among the cups . . .

8. Then fill the cups with the egg mixture, leaving a little space at the top.

9. Set the trivet in the Instant Pot, then carefully pour 1 cup water into the pot.

10. Cover the egg mold snugly with foil and carefully lower it onto the trivet.

11. Secure the lid on the Instant Pot and set the pressure valve to Sealing . . .

12. Then press the Steam button and set it to 10 minutes. (Note that it will take several minutes for the pressure to build, after which the 10-minute timer will automatically start counting down.)

13. After the 10 minutes are up, let the pressure release naturally for 10 minutes, then use the handle of a wooden spoon to move the valve to Venting, which will let the rest of the pressure release quickly.

14. When the pressure is fully released, remove the lid, then remove the silicone mold from the machine. Peel back the foil and turn the egg bites onto a plate. They should pop right out!

15. For the veggie version: In a large skillet, heat the oil over medium heat. Add the mushrooms, broccoli, and bell pepper, then sprinkle with a pinch of salt and pepper.

16. Sauté until the veggies are tender, about 5 minutes. Set aside.

17. Spray a silicone egg mold with cooking spray. In a bowl, whisk the eggs, heavy cream, sour cream, ½ teaspoon salt, and ¼ teaspoon pepper. Divide the Cheddar, veggies, and egg mixture among the cups.

18. Cover snugly with foil and follow the cooking instructions from the chorizo bites.

19. Take them on the run, or freeze them for later!

STANDARD OVEN DIRECTIONS

Preheat the oven to 325°F. Pour water into a 9 x 13-inch baking dish until it's halfway full. Fill the silicone egg tray as above, set it in the pan, and cover the pan with foil. Bake for 1 hour, or until the eggs are set. Let the egg bites sit in the water for 10 minutes before removing them from the mold.

Freezing/ Reheating Instructions

» *Freeze by placing the bites on a lightly greased sheet pan or plate and flash-freeze for 45 minutes. Transfer to a plastic zipper bag and return to the freezer.*

» *To reheat 1 or 2 bites, wrap in a paper towel and microwave for 1 minute. Let sit for 1 minute before eating.*

DUTCH BABY

MAKES 4 TO 6 SERVINGS

WHAT: A ginormous poufy pancake that will wow your guests (and yo'self).

WHEN: Saturday brunch, or any time you want to have a big honkin' pancake for supper!

WHY: Because your guests will want to gather around the oven with their smartphones and record the poufy pancake pandemonium as it happens. What could be more fun?

I don't know what it is about the restaurants I frequented as a child, but they are as tightly woven into the fabric of my history as the perfume I wore and the music I danced to. (Love's Baby Soft, anyone? Duran Duran, anyone?) High on my list of memory-evoking restaurants was Pannekoeken Huis, where servers wearing wooden clogs darted to tables to deliver *pannekoeken* to hungry customers before the pancakes deflated into the skillets they were baked in. No pancake memory holds more excitement for me than that, and I love re-creating the experience at home, sans wooden clogs. Note that the pancake will start to fall as soon as you remove it from the oven, so make sure your recipients are gathered around and won't miss the zany, poufy fun!

3 large eggs

¾ cup whole milk

¾ cup all-purpose flour

1 tablespoon maple syrup, plus more for serving

½ teaspoon vanilla extract

4 tablespoons (½ stick) salted butter, plus more as needed for serving

TOPPINGS

Blueberry jam

Fresh berries

Whipped cream

Powdered sugar

1. Preheat the oven to 425°F. Preheat a 12-inch cast-iron skillet in the oven.

2. In a blender, or in a bowl using an immersion blender, blend the eggs and milk until fluffy.

3. Add the flour, maple syrup, and vanilla . . .

4. And blend until smooth.

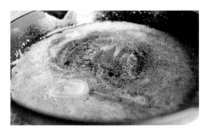

5. Carefully remove the hot skillet from the oven (use heavy-duty hot pads!) and melt the butter in the pan.

6. Acting quickly, pour in the batter and return the pan to the oven.

7. Bake until golden brown and puffy, about 25 minutes. (This is a mere minute after its removal from the oven. It was puffier than this!)

8. While it is still hot, top with butter, jam, berries, and syrup.

9. Slice into wedges and serve with whipped cream, powdered sugar, and more syrup.

Variation

» *Turn the Dutch baby into an ice cream sundae: Pile scoops of ice cream on top and add chocolate syrup, whipped cream, and cherries! Yikes.*

TATER BREAKFAST CASSEROLE

MAKES 8 TO 10 SERVINGS

WHAT: An incredibly cheesy, tater-totty breakfast casserole that you can assemble the night before you need it.

WHEN: When you plan on having a crowd for breakfast. And when that crowd loves cheese.

WHY: Because Tater Tot casseroles are one of the best-kept secrets in gourmet cuisine! Just kidding. But they are so, so good.

It might not look it, but this breakfast casserole is an absolute revelation. It basically checks off all the boxes: It has carbs (Tater Tots). It has protein (sausage). It has color (bell peppers). It is convenient (you can make it the night before). And it is positively loaded with cheese. Also, it is positively loaded with cheese. And yes, I realize I said that twice. But when you see how much cheese is in this casserole, you will understand.

1 pound bulk spicy breakfast sausage

1 medium yellow onion, very finely diced

4 large eggs

1 cup whole milk

½ cup half-and-half

¼ teaspoon seasoned salt, such as Lawry's

¼ teaspoon cayenne pepper

1 red bell pepper, seeded and very finely diced

1 green bell pepper, seeded and very finely diced

2 cups grated Cheddar cheese

1 cup grated pepper Jack cheese

Kosher salt and black pepper

Butter, for the baking dish

One 16-ounce bag frozen Tater Tots

1. In a large skillet, cook the sausage and onion over medium-high heat until browned and cooked through, 8 to 10 minutes.

2. In a large bowl, whisk the eggs, milk, half-and-half, seasoned salt, and cayenne.

3. Add the bell peppers, half of both cheeses, and a pinch each of salt and pepper. Stir and set aside.

4. Butter a 9 x 13-inch baking dish and line it with the frozen tots.

5. Sprinkle the sausage mixture over the tots . . .

6. Followed by the egg–bell pepper–cheese mixture.

7. Spread the mixture evenly over the top . . .

8. And top with the rest of the cheese.

9. Cover the dish with foil and refrigerate overnight. (If you'd like to skip the fridge and go straight to baking, continue on!)

10. When you're ready to bake the casserole, preheat the oven to 350°F. Bake, covered, for 25 minutes, then remove the foil . . .

11. And continue to bake until the cheese is browned and bubbling and the casserole is cooked through, another 25 to 30 minutes.

12. Dig in and serve with cold, refreshing fruit!

CARROT CAKE BAKED FRENCH TOAST

MAKES 8 TO 10 SERVINGS

WHAT: A make-ahead breakfast casserole that tastes like carrot cake!

WHEN: Holidays when all the kids are home, New Year's brunch, slumber party breakfast.

WHY: It seriously tastes like carrot cake. And I like it.

The possibilities for baked French toast are endless, and I've tried probably 943 of them. This carrot cake version was actually thrown together on a whim, when I had a dark, grainy loaf of bread I needed to use. I saw carrots in the fridge, I saw pecans in a canister on my countertop . . . and it all came together in this dastardly dish. It was delicious, but you can make it even better by assembling everything the night before and keeping it in the fridge overnight, then just popping it in the oven for breakfast. It's a winner!

Butter for the dish

1 loaf crusty multigrain bread

1½ cups grated carrots

½ cup finely chopped pecans

8 large eggs

2 cups whole milk

½ cup heavy cream

½ cup granulated sugar

½ cup firmly packed brown sugar

1 tablespoon vanilla extract

½ teaspoon ground cinnamon

TOPPING

½ cup all-purpose flour

½ cup firmly packed brown sugar

Pinch of kosher salt

8 tablespoons (1 stick) cold salted butter, cut into pieces

½ teaspoon ground cinnamon

½ cup finely chopped pecans

GLAZE

4 ounces cream cheese

¾ cup powdered sugar

2 tablespoons milk

1 tablespoon fresh lemon juice

Warm pancake syrup, for serving

1. Grease a 9 x 13-inch baking dish with butter.

2. Tear the bread into large chunks . . .

3. And evenly distribute in the dish.

4. Sprinkle the carrots and pecans over the top. Set aside.

5. In a large bowl, whisk the eggs, milk, cream, granulated sugar, brown sugar, vanilla, and cinnamon.

Tastes just like carrot cake!

6. Pour the mixture over the bread, taking care to coat it all well.

10. And use a pastry cutter to cut the butter into the flour mixture until the mixture resembles pebbles and coarse crumbs.

13. When you're ready to bake the casserole, preheat the oven to 350°F. Remove the foil and sprinkle the topping all over.

7. Cover the pan tightly with foil and keep it in the fridge for several hours or overnight.

11. Stir in the pecans, then cover the bowl and refrigerate the topping until you're ready to bake the French toast.

14. Bake, uncovered, for 50 minutes for a softer, bread pudding–like texture or 70 minutes for a firmer, more crispy baked texture. Remove the glaze from the fridge to allow it to soften.

8. Make the topping: In a large bowl, combine the flour, brown sugar, and salt and mix well.

12. Make the glaze: In the bowl of a stand mixer fitted with the paddle attachment, combine the cream cheese, powdered sugar, milk, and lemon juice and mix until smooth. Transfer to an airtight container and keep it in the fridge until you're ready to serve the French toast.

15. Scoop out individual portions, drizzle the cream cheese glaze on top, and serve with warm pancake syrup.

9. Add the chunks of cold butter and the cinnamon . . .

LOWER-CARB EGGS BENEDICT

MAKES 4 SERVINGS

WHAT: Eggs Benedict with nary an English muffin in sight!

WHEN: For those times you want to cut carbs—and overcompensate with egg yolks.

WHY: Because a poached egg doused with hollandaise is so sublime, you don't care what it is (or isn't) sitting on.

Eggs Benedict is easily one of my top three favorite breakfasts, but it has nothing to do with the toasted English muffin that the poached egg, Canadian bacon, and hollandaise are sitting on. For me, Eggs Benedict is *entirely* about a poached egg with hollandaise. It is a combination that was created in Heaven, and if I live to be four hundred, it will never grow old. And the good news is that it's a pretty acceptable thing to chow down on for breakfast if you're trying to curb carbs! This version calls for a bed of spinach and a little crispy bacon to make it more of a complete dish. Think of me when you cut into that egg, will you? Because you'll be experiencing one of my greatest loves.

6 slices thick-cut bacon, cut in half

2 garlic cloves, minced

One 24-ounce bag baby spinach

Kosher salt and black pepper

4 large eggs

1 teaspoon white vinegar

Cajun Hollandaise (page 229), warmed

1. In a large skillet, cook the bacon over medium-high heat, turning until crisp. Remove from the skillet and drain on a paper towel.

2. Pour off half the grease, reduce the heat to medium-low, and add the garlic. Stir and cook for 30 seconds, taking care not to burn the garlic.

3. Add the spinach, sprinkle with some salt and pepper, and toss.

Hollandaise is happiness!

4. Continue cooking until the spinach is almost totally wilted, about 3 minutes. Set aside and keep warm.

5. To poach the eggs, in a medium saucepan, boil 2 quarts water over medium-high heat. Crack the eggs into separate small ramekins. Set aside.

6. Add a pinch of salt and the vinegar.

7. Use a metal spoon to carefully stir a vigorous whirlpool into the water . . .

8. Then immediately drop one of the eggs into the center of the whirlpool . . .

9. And let it cook for about 3 minutes for a soft yolk.

10. Use a slotted spoon to carefully lift the egg out of the water. Gently shake the spoon and check the doneness. If the egg is too soft, return it to the water for 45 seconds. Repeat with the other eggs. (You can poach two at a time if you prefer!)

11. Divide the spinach among four plates. Top the spinach with 3 slices of bacon, then place an egg on top of the bacon.

12. Pour on the hollandaise and serve!

Cows and clouds!

"Is it lunchtime yet?"

Lunch

Lunch is an interesting and thought-provoking mealtime! Its lines are sometimes blurred, and it can sometimes take on an "anything goes" identity. In fact, at any given midday meal, you're liable to find me eating anything from French toast to pot roast—and that's exactly what I love about lunch. However, you can't beat a good ol' sandwich, and you'll find a handful of great ones in the next several pages! (Warning: They are not small. Additional warning: They are large.) I also include a couple of soups (hot and cold!) and a gorgeous fruit salad that will beg you to invite some lunch company over (even if the salad's in Tupperware and you invite coworkers to your lunch table!). Embrace lunch, friends. It's low-key, low-stress, and all about celebrating that tried-and-true institution known as *lunch*!

A cool, colorful salad!

TOMATO, WATERMELON, AND FETA SALAD

MAKES 8 TO 12 SERVINGS

WHAT: A bright, colorful, refreshing salad.

WHEN: Summertime! It's a beauty!

WHY: The huge chunks of tomato, watermelon, and feta are dramatic and delicious!

My mother-in-law, Nan, loved her dad's legendary garden, and she always proclaimed his fruits and vegetables to be the freshest she ever ate in her life. Especially anchored in her memories were his tomatoes and watermelons; she described them in such vivid and juicy detail that my mouth would water just listening to her. In the week after we lost Nan, I made this salad in celebration of all her stories of her father's garden . . . and of Nan herself. We miss her so much.

½ seedless watermelon

6 to 8 beautiful ripe tomatoes (any color!)

¼ cup olive oil

2 tablespoons fresh lemon juice

1 tablespoon honey

¼ teaspoon kosher salt

Pinch of black pepper

One 8-ounce block feta cheese, cut into 1-inch cubes

12 basil leaves, mix of torn and whole

3 tablespoons balsamic glaze

1. Cut the rind off the watermelon half, then cut the fruit into 1½-inch chunks. Slice the tomatoes into large wedges.

2. In a small jar, combine the olive oil, lemon juice, honey, salt, and pepper. Put the lid on the jar and shake it up.

3. In a large bowl, combine the watermelon and tomatoes. Pour on three-quarters of the dressing . . .

4. And toss to coat.

6. Arrange the salad on a platter with the basil on top . . .

7. Then add the balsamic glaze in a pretty zigzag pattern.

5. Add the feta and toss carefully to keep the cheese intact.

Variations

» *Substitute any melon for the watermelon.*

» *Add very thinly sliced red onion to the salad for a little extra flavor.*

Working calves together as a family. The best way to work calves!

EGG-IN-A-HOLE SANDWICH

MAKES 1 GENEROUS SANDWICH (TO SERVE 2)

WHAT: A honkin' breakfast sandwich made with two honkin' egg-in-a-holes!

WHEN: Portable breakfast, casual brunch.

WHY: Because sometimes it's just fun to build a sandwich you can't fit your mouth around.

Egg-in-a-holes have been a favorite Drummond breakfast for generations. Ladd's grandmother made them for him any time he visited her house, whether it was breakfast time or not, and so it was only fitting that when I set out to create the most outrageous breakfast sandwich I could possibly make, egg-in-a-holes would be the star of the show. I used thick, generous slices of bread for this one, but you can keep things in moderation and just use regular sandwich bread. (Yes, I can hear you laughing at my use of the word "moderation.")

4 tablespoons (½ stick) salted butter

1 thick-cut ham steak

1 round loaf rustic bread

2 extra-large eggs

Kosher salt and black pepper

¼ cup mayonnaise

1 to 2 tablespoons jalapeño hot sauce (or regular hot sauce)

3 slices pepper Jack cheese

Green leaf lettuce

2 Roma tomatoes, sliced

1. In a large cast-iron skillet, melt 1 tablespoon of the butter over medium-high heat. Fry the ham steak on both sides until browned, about 2 minutes per side. Remove it from the skillet and set it aside. Reduce the heat to medium-low.

3. Use a 4-inch biscuit cutter or the rim of a large cup to cut out a round in the center of each slice of bread.

5. Then add both slices of bread (as well as the cut-out holes), swirling them around to absorb the butter and then turning them over.

2. Cut two similar-size slices from the center of the round loaf. (I used sourdough.)

4. Add 2 more tablespoons of the butter to the skillet and let it melt . . .

6. Crack an egg into each hole, season with salt and pepper, and let them cook until the eggs start to set, 1½ to 2 minutes.

7. Using a spatula, carefully flip the bread with the egg, then season the other side with salt and pepper. Add the remaining tablespoon butter to the skillet if needed and cook until the second side is set, about 1½ minutes.

8. Remove the egg-in-a-holes to a plate or board and let them sit while you prepare the sandwich spread.

9. In a small bowl, mix together the mayonnaise and hot sauce. Season with salt and pepper.

10. Spread a generous amount on each egg-in-a-hole . . .

11. Add the cheese slices to one egg-in-a-hole, slightly overlapping them.

12. Add the ham . . .

13. The lettuce and tomato slices . . .

14. And the other egg-in-a-hole!

15. Slice down the middle and go for it! Just make sure you have a friend to help ya.

Variations

» Substitute cooked bacon slices or cooked sausage patties for the ham.

» Use Cheddar, Swiss, provolone, or any cheese you'd like!

» Give things a little twist by using cinnamon-raisin bread instead. (Trust me!)

What a thing of beauty!

CHICKEN "NEW"-DLE SOUP

MAKES 8 SERVINGS

WHAT: Classic, comforting chicken noodle soup updated with butternut squash and kale.

WHEN: Lunch on a cold winter day, supper on a cold winter night, delivery to a new mom, soup potluck.

WHY: Because you can't beat the classics . . . but you can give them yummy tweaks!

I am, hilariously, married to a nonsoup humanoid. I say "hilariously" because I happen to love soup, and it is a continual source of culinary frustration to me that Ladd doesn't relish the thousands—nay, *millions* of varieties of soup there are in the world. But it's true. Soup just doesn't make Ladd tick.

There is one exception: chicken noodle soup. He loves it. Yes, the most basic, run-of-the-mill soup in the universe is the one my husband has settled on. Fortunately (let's bring this back to me), I love it, too—especially when I can sneak in a few variations here and there. Emphasis on "sneak." (Hello, butternut squash and kale!)

4 boneless, skinless chicken thighs

Kosher salt and black pepper

2 tablespoons olive oil

1 medium onion, finely diced

3 purple (or regular orange) carrots, peeled, halved, and sliced crosswise

½ butternut squash, peeled and cut into ½-inch cubes (about 2 cups)

2 celery stalks, thinly sliced

1 garlic clove, minced

1 tablespoon minced fresh thyme leaves

1 teaspoon fresh oregano leaves

⅛ teaspoon ground turmeric

6 cups low-sodium chicken broth

3 cups cooked egg noodles

2 cups stemmed and chopped kale

1. Season the chicken on both sides with salt and pepper.

2. In a Dutch oven, heat the olive oil over medium-high heat. Add the chicken and cook on one side for 3 minutes . . .

3. Then flip it over and cook until the chicken is cooked through, another 3 minutes. Remove the chicken from the pot and set it aside.

4. Reduce the heat to medium, add the onion, carrots, squash, celery, and garlic to the pot . . .

5. And cook, stirring occasionally, until starting to soften, 2 to 3 minutes.

6. Add the thyme, oregano, and turmeric. Stir and cook until the veggies are starting to turn color, 3 to 4 minutes.

7. Pour in the broth, increase the heat to medium-high, and bring to a gentle boil.

8. Dice the chicken into small pieces . . .

9. Then add it to the pot and stir it in. Reduce the heat to low and simmer until the vegetables are tender, about 20 minutes. Remove the pot from the heat, then taste and adjust the seasoning.

10. To serve, place about ⅓ cup noodles in a bowl . . .

11. And add ¼ cup kale.

12. Ladle the hot soup on top and serve!

Variation

» Omit the noodles for a straight-up chicken-and-kale soup.

BACON, KALE, AND TOMATO SANDWICH

MAKES 1 GENEROUS SANDWICH (TO SERVE 2)

WHAT: A fabulously flavorful sandwich that will make you forget boring ol' lettuce ever existed.

WHEN: Weekday lunch, weekend lunch, late-afternoon lunch, midnight lunch . . . you get the idea.

WHY: Because kale is good for you, no matter what accompanies it!

I once substituted raw kale for lettuce in my go-to BLT, and while it was a pretty nice variation, my taste buds craved something more. So the next time (also known as the next day), I quick-cooked the kale and added a little touch of apple cider vinegar to brighten things up. It was a miracle! (A mashed avocado and a creamy pesto mayo didn't hurt, either . . .)

6 slices bacon

3 tablespoons salted butter

4 large curly kale leaves, stemmed and torn in half

1 tablespoon apple cider vinegar

2 teaspoons honey

Kosher salt and black pepper

2 slices country bread

1 large avocado, pitted

2 tablespoons mayonnaise

1 tablespoon prepared pesto, store-bought or homemade (see page 161)

1 medium tomato, sliced thick

1. Fry the bacon until crisp. Remove and drain on a paper towel.

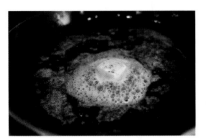

2. Pour off the excess grease from the skillet. Return it to medium heat and add 1 tablespoon of the butter.

3. When the butter is melted, add the kale . . .

4. Along with the vinegar. Stir to cook for 1 minute.

5. Add the honey and a sprinkle of salt and pepper . . .

6. And cook, stirring, until it's partially wilted, about 2 more minutes. Remove to a plate.

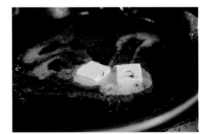

7. Without wiping or cleaning the skillet, add the remaining 2 tablespoons butter to melt.

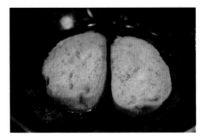

8. Add the two slices of bread, moving them around the pan so that they absorb most of the butter, and cook until golden on the first side.

9. Flip the slices and cook the other side until golden. Remove the bread from the pan.

10. Scoop the avocado into a small bowl and mash with a fork.

11. In another small bowl, stir together the mayonnaise and pesto.

12. To assemble the sandwich, spread the pesto mayo on both pieces of bread.

13. Spread the avocado on top of both pieces.

17. Top it with the other piece of bread . . .

18. Then add a toothpick to each half and slice.

14. Shingle the tomato slices on the bottom slice and sprinkle them with salt and pepper.

15. Add the bacon slices on top of the tomatoes . . .

16. And finally, the kale on top of the bacon!

Variations

» *Substitute shaved turkey or ham for the bacon.*

» *Omit the meat for a vegetarian sandwich.*

» *Substitute Swiss chard or collard greens for the kale.*

» *Mix the mayo with chopped chipotle peppers instead of pesto for a nice kick.*

I can't decide who's cuter.

FRIED TOMATO SANDWICH

MAKES 1 LARGE SANDWICH (TO SERVE 2)

WHAT: A big, beautiful sandwich with crispy fried tomatoes and fresh basil.

WHEN: Lunchtime, or a summertime dinner.

WHY: Because green tomatoes aren't the only ones that can be fried!

Let's get this out of the way: I love the movie *Fried Green Tomatoes*. It makes me laugh, it makes me cry, and it's the reason I declare that "I'm older and I have more insurance" at least once a month when someone is challenging me about something and I don't feel like explaining myself. It's also the reason that fried green tomatoes took root in my consciousness and became a favorite to cook whenever I found myself with a random pile of unripe tomatoes from my garden. But through the years, I've found that fried tomatoes are good whether they're green, red, yellow, purple, or any color in between. And making a sandwich out of them is something I will continue to do, and do you know why? Because I'm older and I have more insurance.

Vegetable oil, for frying

1 large, firm heirloom tomato

⅓ cup ground cornmeal

2 tablespoons cornstarch

1 teaspoon kosher salt, plus more for sprinkling

½ teaspoon black pepper, plus more for sprinkling

1 large egg

2 tablespoons salted butter

2 thick slices sourdough bread

2 tablespoons mayonnaise

Handful of basil leaves

1. Pour ¼ inch oil into a large skillet over medium heat.

2. Cut the tomato into three thick slices. (You can see that I cheated and used 2 colors of tomatoes.)

3. In a shallow dish, combine the cornmeal, cornstarch, salt, and pepper . . .

4. And whisk to combine.

5. Whisk the egg in a separate bowl.

6. Place one of the tomato slices in the cornmeal mixture . . .

7. And flip it over to coat.

8. Immediately dunk it in the egg and turn it over to coat.

9. Then return it to the cornmeal mixture and coat both sides again.

10. Check that the oil is the right temperature by dropping in a pinch of cornmeal. It should sizzle but not turn brown immediately. Carefully use a spatula to place the tomatoes in the oil.

11. Fry the tomatoes until the coating is golden, about 1½ minutes, then gently turn them over (be careful not to splash the hot oil!).

12. When the second side is golden, place the tomatoes on a paper towel to drain.

13. In a separate skillet, melt the butter over medium heat. Add the bread and toast it until golden on both sides.

14. Spread both slices of toast with mayonnaise, then sprinkle with salt and pepper.

15. Lay on the fried tomatoes . . .

16. Then top the other piece of bread with the basil leaves.

17. Place the second piece of bread on top, basil side down.

18. Slice the sandwich in half . . .

19. And share! But only if you can part with 50 percent of this perfection.

Variations

» *Lay 3 fried bacon slices on top of the tomatoes.*

» *Add a generous pile of arugula or spinach on top of the tomatoes.*

MOVIE FOOD

I remember food I've seen in movies as much as I remember the plotlines and the acting. Here are some of my most cherished movie food memories:

✿ Spaghetti carbonara in *Heartburn*

✿ Pizza in *Mystic Pizza*

✿ Boeuf bourguignon in *Julie & Julia*

✿ Turkey Marbella in *Scent of a Woman*

✿ Clemenza's sauce in *The Godfather*

✿ Strudel in *Shining Through*

✿ Schnitzel with noodles in *The Sound of Music*

✿ Turkish Delight in *The Lion, the Witch and the Wardrobe*

✿ Marshmallow creme in *Ghostbusters*

✿ Pastrami on rye in *When Harry Met Sally*

✿ Caviar garnish in *You've Got Mail*

✿ Razzles in *13 Going on 30*

HONEYDEW GAZPACHO

MAKES 8 SERVINGS

WHAT: Cold green soup. I don't know how else to say it. (It's amazing!)

WHEN: Luncheon with girlfriends or a summertime starter. (Serve it in shot glasses!)

WHY: Because green gazpacho is the road less traveled—and when it comes to food, that can be an amazing thing!

Cold soup can be an adjustment for those who aren't used to such madness, but once you dive into a generous bowl of chilled gazpacho on a hot summer day, things begin to make perfect sense. But just when you think you've gotten used to a more typical gazpacho—which is customarily tomato-based, almost like a salsa you can eat with a spoon—some rabble-rousing redhead comes along and asks you to accept a version in (egads!) bright green.

You know how redheads are about green. It's our favorite color! So try this soup in our honor.

It's green and glorious!

1 small honeydew melon, peeled, seeded, and roughly chopped

1 large cucumber, peeled, halved lengthwise, seeded, and roughly chopped

1 cup green grapes

1 cup packed spinach leaves

¼ cup basil leaves

4 green onions, sliced

1 serrano pepper, seeded and chopped

2 tablespoons olive oil

1 tablespoon Champagne vinegar

Juice of 1 lime

1 tablespoon honey

1 avocado, halved

½ teaspoon kosher salt

½ teaspoon black pepper

¼ cup cilantro leaves, for serving

4 lime wedges, for serving

1. Place the honeydew in a food processor. Look at that gorgeous green!

5. Pulse a few more times, then add the olive oil, vinegar, lime juice, and honey. Process until pureed, about 30 seconds. The mixture will be chunky.

8. Ladle the soup into bowls. I love the contrasting colors!

2. Pulse it a few times to make room for the other ingredients.

6. Scoop in half of the avocado, add the salt and pepper, and pulse once or twice to combine.

9. Slice the remaining avocado half and top the soup with sliced avocado and cilantro leaves. Serve with lime wedges!

3. Add the cucumber and grapes . . .

7. Thin with ice water if necessary to reach the desired consistency. Transfer to a bowl, cover, and refrigerate for at least 1 hour.

Variations

» *Add 2 or 3 grilled shrimp to the top of each bowl of soup.*

» *Add a jalapeño along with the serrano for more heat.*

» *Top with mango salsa if you'd like to add more color.*

4. And the spinach, basil, green onions, and serrano pepper.

ENGLISH MUFFIN GRILLED CHEESE

MAKES 1 SANDWICH, TO SERVE 2

WHAT: A stacked-to-the-sky grilled cheese made with an English muffin, cheese, and all the fixins.

WHEN: When you're in the mood for an outrageous sandwich, and you have someone to share it with. This one's huge!

WHY: Because the English muffin is grilled inside out, which makes the surface a crispy dream. (Oh, and there's bacon in it.)

A grilled cheese sandwich is one of those rare dishes that's as good in its original form as in all its varied forms. On any given day, I could be more than happy with a grilled cheese made from soft white bread and American cheese. But I could be equally happy (as you can imagine) with a grilled cheese like this one, that boasts five (yes, five!) different cheeses along with other fillings. The English muffin standing in as the bread is something out of a dream! Its surface crisps up, and it becomes so different from the butter-and-jam English muffin you know and love. Try this next time a grilled cheese sounds good to you.

5 sandwich-size cheese slices (I used Colby Jack, provolone, sharp Cheddar, pepper Jack, and Gouda, but you can use all the same cheese or mix it up as you wish!)

2 slices bacon, cut in half and fried

2 thin tomato slices

2 thin red onion slices

½ avocado, sliced

1 English muffin, split

2 tablespoons salted butter

1. Preheat the oven to 350°F. Heat an ovenproof skillet over medium-low heat.

2. Lay out the cheeses . . .

3. Then lay out the bacon, tomato, onion, and avocado in the same way.

4. Place one English muffin half on a board cut side down. Beginning with 1 slice of cheese, alternate cheese and other ingredients. It's like shuffling a tasty deck of cards! Top with the second English muffin half cut side up.

5. Melt the butter in the skillet and carefully place the sandwich right on the butter so that it's absorbed by the English muffin. Cook for about 5 minutes, checking to make sure it doesn't burn.

6. Carefully flip it over, then place the skillet in the oven. Toast the sandwich in the oven until the cheese is fully melted, about 5 minutes.

7. Use a serrated knife to slice it in half . . . and dig in!

EGG SALAD EGGS-PLOSION

MAKES 6 TO 8 SERVINGS OF 3 VARIETIES (18 TO 24 SERVINGS TOTAL)

WHAT: A trio of terrific egg salads.

WHEN: Lunch for the ladies, munchies for the men, or snacktime.

WHY: Because egg salad is an underrated joy on earth and I want to bring it back with a vengeance.

Egg salad needn't be relegated to the day after Easter, as a way of using up hard-boiled eggs. On the contrary, it should be celebrated! Venerated! Exalted! And . . . uh . . . gobbled up. I really think a plate of egg salad makes the perfect lunch, but it's also a great snack at any time of day if you're looking for something low-carb and luscious. Here, I take a good-size batch of my very-basic-but-beautiful egg salad and turn it into three distinctly different versions. The variety is gorgeous!

BASIC EGG SALAD

24 large eggs, hard-boiled (see page 75), peeled, and roughly chopped

1 cup mayonnaise

2 tablespoons Dijon mustard

1 tablespoon white vinegar

1 teaspoon hot sauce

2 tablespoons heavy cream

Kosher salt and black pepper

VEGGIE-TASTIC VERSION

½ cup finely diced celery

½ cup pickled red onions (see page 177)

½ cup diced tomato

One 2-ounce jar diced pimientos, drained

SPICY SRIRACHA VERSION

2 tablespoons sriracha sauce

¼ cup roughly chopped cilantro leaves

½ cup chopped sweet pickles

COBB VERSION

2 heaping tablespoons prepared pesto, store-bought or homemade (see page 161)

1 avocado, diced

3 slices bacon, fried until crisp and chopped into small pieces

¼ cup finely chopped sun-dried tomatoes

1 tablespoon roughly chopped dill, plus more for garnish

Juice of ½ lemon

FOR SERVING

Butter lettuce leaves

Endive leaves

Radicchio leaves

1. First, make the base egg salad: Place the chopped eggs in a large bowl and set it aside.

3. Pour the dressing over the eggs . . .

2. In a separate bowl, combine the mayonnaise, Dijon, vinegar, hot sauce, cream, and 1 teaspoon each salt and pepper. Stir until well combined.

4. And fold gently until the dressing totally coats the eggs. Take a bite and add more salt and pepper if it needs it.

"This looks EGG-cellent!"

5. Now comes the fun part! Divide the base egg salad into three separate bowls.

8. For the Spicy Sriracha version: Add the sriracha, cilantro, and pickles to the second bowl . . .

11. And stir until combined. Taste and adjust the seasonings.

6. For the Veggie-tastic version: Add the celery, pickled red onions, tomato, and pimientos to the first bowl . . .

9. And stir until combined. Taste and add more of whatever you think it needs.

12. Serve the egg salads in lettuce, endive, and radicchio leaves.

7. And stir until combined. Taste and adjust the seasoning as needed.

10. For the Cobb version: Add the pesto, avocado, bacon, sun-dried tomatoes, dill, and lemon juice to the third bowl . . .

They're all *eggs-cellent*!

PERFECT HARD-BOILED EGGS: ON THE STOVETOP

1. Place the eggs in a saucepan or pot. You can do as few as 1 or as many as 12!

3. Then place the lid on the pot, turn the heat to medium-high, and bring to a boil.

5. When they're completely chilled (5 minutes), use the spoon to tap around the shell . . .

2. Cover the eggs in cold water by 1 inch . . .

4. Boil for exactly 8 minutes, then immediately plunge the eggs into ice water.

6. And peel it right off! Super easy.

PERFECT HARD-BOILED EGGS: IN AN INSTANT POT

1. Place the rack in the bottom of the Instant Pot insert and add a single layer of eggs (again, up to 12).

3. Then set the Instant Pot to Manual for 5 minutes. (It will take a few minutes to build pressure first.)

5. And plunge the eggs into ice water as above.

2. Pour in 1 cup of water and put the lid on . . .

4. When the 5 minutes are up, use a spoon to push the valve to Venting. When the steam is fully released, remove the lid . . .

They turn out perfect every time—no matter which method you use!

"This is my happy face."

Snacks and Starters

My ideal meal is not a meal at all, but an array of smaller appetizers in various vessels laid out in front of me. If I stand up when I eat them, even better: The calories won't count! Just kidding (I don't want to get in trouble here). But what I'm saying is, I just love a good snack. These are some of my current faves, some of which are lower in carbs! And some of which are not . . .

A great
lower-carb
munchie!

PARMESAN CRISPS, TWO WAYS

MAKES 12 CRISPS, FOR 4 TO 6 SERVINGS

WHAT: Thin and crispy rounds of baked Parmesan cheese.

WHEN: A party munchie, an afternoon snack, or an accompaniment to salad.

WHY: They're a low-carb alternative to crackers or chips. Addictive!

I became hooked on Parmesan crisps when I embarked on a low-carb fest a year or so ago and was buying so many of them that I finally gave in and started making my own. For one thing, the closest place I could procure the crunchy little wonders was in Tulsa, an hour and a half from our house on the ranch. For another, I grew so fond of them that the fear of running out of them on any given day was a frightening thought. For yet another, they happen to be the easiest snack in the world to make—and you can top them with a bite of jalapeño or a hit of seasoning . . . or you can leave them plain and unadorned. (Pssst. You don't have to be on a low-carb kick to love them!)

1 teaspoon poppy seeds

1 teaspoon white sesame seeds, toasted (see Note)

1 teaspoon black sesame seeds

½ teaspoon dried minced garlic

½ teaspoon dried minced onion

1 cup freshly shredded Parmesan cheese (use the large holes of the grater)

6 jarred pickled jalapeño slices

Soft-spread herbed cheese, for serving (optional)

1. Preheat the oven to 400°F. Line a sheet pan with parchment paper or a baking mat.

2. Make the everything seasoning: In a small bowl, mix together the poppy seeds, toasted sesame seeds, garlic, and onion. Set aside.

3. Using a tablespoon, measure 12 rounded piles of the Parmesan onto the baking sheet.

4. Place a jalapeño slice on 6 of the piles. Bake until the cheese has melted into flat discs and they start to turn golden, 10 to 11 minutes.

5. Remove them from the oven and immediately sprinkle the everything seasoning over the other 6 crisps before they start to set. Press very lightly to set the seasoning.

6. Let them cool to room temperature. They'll crisp up as they cool!

7. Serve them as is, or with soft-spread herbed cheese. Store them in an airtight container for up to 5 days.

Note: To toast the sesame seeds, place them in a dry skillet over low heat and toast for a few minutes, stirring often, until lightly browned.

Variations

» *Place a large olive slice in the middle of each crisp.*

» *Mix the Parmesan with Cheddar, Gruyère, or other hard/firm cheeses to change up the flavors.*

» *Mix the cheese with ½ teaspoon chili powder to give it a kick.*

PARMESAN CRISPS: THEY'RE SWEEPING THE NATION!

Here are a few fun ways to use them:

✿ Place 1 crisp on top of a cup of tomato soup.

✿ Add 2 to 3 crisps to your salad for a little protein and crunch.

✿ Lay a couple of crisps inside your favorite cold cut sandwich.

✿ Use the crisps as a base for bruschetta topping: Top them with diced tomatoes, basil, and balsamic, or a little olive tapenade!

✿ Immediately after removing them from the oven, use a sharp-edged spatula to quickly lay them over mini-muffin cups. Allow them to naturally sink down into the cups, helping them with your fingers if necessary. Let them set, then fill them with toppings or fillings of your choice.

✿ Immediately after removing them from the oven, use a sharp-edged spatula to drape them over a wooden dowel (or handle of a large wooden spoon). Let them set, and you'll have Parmesan crisp taco shells!

✿ Make smaller, coin-size crisps by using smaller piles of Parmesan and baking them for 4 to 5 minutes. Sprinkle them as croutons or snack on them liberally!

SALSA VERDE

MAKES ABOUT 2 CUPS

WHAT: Delightful green salsa.

WHEN: When you want to show your guests how gorgeous salsa can be!

WHY: Because life's too short to enjoy one color of salsa at a time.

There is nothing smooth and simple about this ultrachunky, bright green salsa! It boasts the spice of jalapeños and little bits of roasted skin from poblanos and tomatillos. Spike the whole thing with a big handful of cilantro and you have varying shades of green and extreme levels of flavor that will make you want to stock your kitchen with all the ingredients so you can whip this up whenever you get the urge. Which, I'll warn you, will be every day at 4:30. (I'm speaking from experience here.) Store this in the fridge and serve it with chips, enchiladas, quesadillas, or tacos!

1½ pounds tomatillos, husked and quartered

1 medium yellow onion, peeled and quartered

2 jalapeños, stemmed, quartered lengthwise, and partially seeded

3 poblano peppers, stemmed, halved lengthwise, and seeded

5 garlic cloves, peeled

2 tablespoons olive oil

Kosher salt

1 cup cilantro leaves

Juice of 1 lime

1. Preheat the oven to 425°F.

2. Place the tomatillos, onion, jalapeños, poblanos, and garlic on a sheet pan.

4. Place the pan in the oven and roast until everything is soft and starting to brown, 15 to 17 minutes. Let cool for 20 minutes.

3. Drizzle on the olive oil and sprinkle with salt. Toss to coat.

5. Place the contents of the pan in a food processor (don't worry about peeling the peppers!) . . .

6. Then add the cilantro and lime juice.

7. Pulse a few times, just until everything is evenly broken up but still very chunky.

8. Taste and adjust the salt!

Engagement Fiesta!

Alex and I threw a Mexican-themed fiesta for her BFF, Meg . . . who happens to be the daughter of my BBF, Hyacinth! Salsa was in attendance. Here's to Meg and Stephen, and here's to love!

SALSA ROJA

MAKES ABOUT 3½ CUPS

WHAT: A deep red, smoky, sexy, all-purpose salsa. (Yes, I just called salsa sexy. What's that all about?)

WHEN: Any time you need salsa in your life! Appetizers, snacks, tacos, enchiladas, salads.

WHY: Because this is different from the typical salsa that dots the landscape. You'll taste its uniqueness!

I was about to write that this is more of a sauce than a salsa, but then I reminded myself that the literal translation of *salsa* is "sauce." So I guess what I am trying to say is that this smooth, chunk-free salsa is set apart from the regular stuff into which we're all used to dipping our tortilla chips. It's made with dried guajillo chiles, which have become my best friends in recent years due to their mild-but-mysterious flavor. I love making this salsa! Having it in the fridge is one of the secrets to my happiness.

6 ounces dried guajillo chiles (found in the Hispanic or international foods aisle), stemmed

8 garlic cloves, peeled

1 medium white or yellow onion, thinly sliced

½ cup chopped cilantro leaves

One 14.5-ounce can diced fire-roasted tomatoes

3 tablespoons olive oil

Juice of 1 lime

½ teaspoon kosher salt

¼ teaspoon black pepper

1. In a medium Dutch oven, combine the chiles, garlic, onion, and cilantro.

3. Bring the water to a boil over medium-high heat, then let it boil for 1 to 2 minutes. Remove the pan from the heat and cover.

5. Transfer the contents of the pot to a blender . . .

2. Pour in enough water to cover the ingredients, 5 to 6 cups.

4. Let it sit until the chiles are soft and the liquid has cooled to lukewarm, about 45 minutes.

6. And blend until well combined, about 1 minute.

7. Add the tomatoes and olive oil . . .

9. Set a fine-mesh strainer over the Dutch oven and pour in the sauce.

11. Bring the liquid to a boil over medium-high heat, then reduce the heat and simmer for 10 minutes.

8. Then blend for another 30 seconds.

10. Use a spoon or spatula to slowly force all the liquid into the pot. Discard the pulp.

12. Remove from the heat and let the salsa cool completely, then add the lime juice, salt, and pepper.

I can't get enough of this!

13. Store in an airtight container in the fridge for up to 2 weeks. Enjoy with chips or anything that needs a little kick!

These give zucchini "bread"
a whole new meaning!

ZUCCHINI CAPRESE SLIDERS

MAKES 12 SLIDERS

WHAT: Zucchini, tomato, and mozzarella mini-sandwiches.

WHEN: A summer party, a light lunch, heck—a super-light dinner!

WHY: Because if you didn't know zucchini slices could be used as a bun, you've been livin' in the dark, pookie head.

During the occasional periods of my life when I am trying to cut carbs, I will go to great lengths to pretend I'm not cutting carbs. Case in point: these little veggie sandwiches. The first time I made them, I actually tried to convince myself they were like most other sandwiches, made with carb-y, heavenly bread. But then, after the first bite, I realized there wasn't a crumb of bread in sight . . . and I didn't actually miss it, because these little slider-style sandwiches were *soooo* good! I've been a believer ever since.

2 large zucchini	5 Roma tomatoes	2 splashes red wine vinegar
2 tablespoons olive oil	½ cup mayonnaise	24 medium or 12 large basil leaves
Kosher salt and black pepper	3 tablespoons prepared pesto, store-bought or homemade (see page 161)	Balsamic glaze, for drizzling
12 ounces fresh mozzarella cheese		

1. Heat a grill pan over medium heat.

2. Slice each zucchini on a diagonal into 12 slices, about ⅓ inch thick.

3. Brush one side of the zucchini with olive oil and season with salt and pepper.

4. Place the slices oil side down on the pan and cook for about 2 minutes, until they have grill marks on the bottom.

5. Turn them over and grill until they have grill marks on the other side but are still somewhat firm. Set them aside to cool.

6. Cut the mozzarella into 12 rounds, then cut each round in half.

7. Cut the tomatoes into 24 slices.

8. Next, make the dressing: In a small bowl, combine the mayonnaise, pesto, and vinegar. Stir until smooth.

9. To assemble, top a slice of zucchini with a layer of the dressing.

10. Arrange two of the half-moons of mozzarella so that they fit the zucchini. Arrange 2 tomato slices on top and sprinkle with salt and pepper.

11. Top with 1 or 2 basil leaves, then drizzle on some glaze.

12. Top with another zucchini slice and secure with a toothpick.

13. Assemble the other sliders and serve!

MAKE-AHEAD

While the sliders are best assembled just before serving, you can get the components ready up to 24 hours before your gathering. Make the dressing and slice the tomatoes and mozzarella, then store them in separate containers in the fridge. Go ahead and grill the zucchini slices, too, then arrange them in a container, separating layers with waxed paper. All ready to go!

BLUEBERRY-RICOTTA CROSTINI

MAKES 16 CROSTINI

WHAT: Crisp, buttery toasts topped with creamy ricotta and sweet balsamic blueberries. Dang!

WHEN: A summer cocktail party, a movie night with friends, or any time you have a food snob over to your house.

WHY: They look so impressive but are so simple to make. Win-win!

My favorite food is anything that you can eat standing up. And I know, I know—you can eat any food standing up. But . . . nibbles. Treats. Snacks. Lighter fare. I mean . . . when's the last time you devoured a pan of lasagna while standing up? (Oh . . . just yesterday? Never mind. And me too, by the way.) Anyway, these beautiful bites are just bursting with summer goodness, no matter what time of year you enjoy them. They're sure to make an impression.

8 tablespoons (1 stick) salted butter, softened

1 small loaf soft French bread, sliced into sixteen ½-inch-thick rounds

1 pint fresh blueberries

2 tablespoons sugar

1 tablespoon balsamic vinegar

1½ cups whole-milk ricotta cheese

¼ cup heavy cream

Zest and juice of 1 lemon, plus more zest for serving

Kosher salt and black pepper

Balsamic glaze, for serving

Small basil leaves (or chiffonade of basil), for serving

1. Preheat the oven to 400°F.

2. Prepare the crostini by spreading ½ tablespoon butter on each slice of bread.

3. Lay the bread on a sheet pan and toast it until slightly crisp and golden brown, about 10 minutes. Set aside to cool completely.

4. In a medium bowl, combine the blueberries and sugar . . .

5. Add the balsamic vinegar . . .

9. Process the mixture until very smooth and slightly fluffy, about 2 minutes.

13. Then top with basil and some more lemon zest.

6. And stir until combined. Let sit to macerate while you prepare the other ingredients.

10. To build the crostini, smear a heaping tablespoon of the ricotta mixture on a toast . . .

Variations

» *Substitute small halved strawberries for the blueberries.*

» *Substitute cream cheese and/or goat cheese (or a mixture thereof) for the ricotta.*

» *Toast larger slices of sourdough bread and serve as breakfast toast!*

7. In a food processor, combine the ricotta and cream . . .

11. And top with a spoonful of the blueberries. Repeat to make the rest.

FROZEN IS FINE!

If you don't have fresh blueberries on hand, just thaw 2 cups of frozen ones in a small colander placed in the sink, then mix them with the sugar and balsamic as directed. Frozen blueberries hold their shape beautifully!

8. The lemon zest, half the lemon juice, and a dash each of salt and pepper.

12. Transfer the crostini to a plate or serving platter. Drizzle with some balsamic glaze . . .

GREEK GUACAMOLE

MAKES 6 TO 8 SERVINGS

WHAT: Good ol' guacamole with a Mediterranean spin!

WHEN: Football party, casual get-together, movie night.

WHY: Because any guacamole is delicious . . . but this takes things to the next level.

I never knew guacamole could be anything other than a heavenly Mexican dip . . . and strictly speaking, it probably can't be. I love traditional guacamole so much, it's hard to imagine changing it up . . . but then I made a Michigander friend named Sheila, and she introduced me to this crazy-flavorful Greek version. Instead of the south-of-the-border flavors I'm in love with, this boasts briny olives and delicious feta cheese. And while the original will always be my first love, I like to "cheat" with this version from time to time. It's addictive!

3 large avocados, diced

1 garlic clove

2 Roma tomatoes, diced

¼ cup finely diced red onion

¼ cup finely chopped jarred roasted red peppers

¼ cup finely chopped pitted kalamata olives

¼ cup chopped parsley

3 tablespoons chopped dill

¼ teaspoon ground cumin

½ teaspoon kosher salt

Juice of 1 lemon

¾ cup crumbled feta cheese, plus more for serving

4 pita breads, each cut into 6 wedges, for serving

Root vegetable chips (such as Terra Chips), for serving

1. In a large bowl, mash the avocado about halfway. You still want some big chunks!

2. Using a Microplane zester, grate in the garlic.

3. Add the tomatoes, onion, roasted peppers, olives, parsley, and dill.

GUACAMOLE FUSION! (JUST ADD TO MASHED AVOCADO)

Asian Fusion: Wasabi paste, minced ginger, lime. Drizzle with sriracha. Serve with wonton chips.

American Fusion: Crumbled bacon, diced hard-boiled egg and tomato, blue cheese crumbles. Serve with pita chips.

Caribbean Fusion: Diced mango, red onion, and red bell pepper. Serve with plantain chips.

4. Sprinkle in the cumin and salt. Squeeze in the lemon . . .

5. And stir everything together until combined.

6. Add the feta and fold it in.

7. Top with additional feta and serve with pita wedges and root vegetable chips. (And a glass of white wine!)

GOAT CHEESE TRUFFLES

MAKES ABOUT 24 TRUFFLES

WHAT: Diminutive balls of creamy goat cheese coated in color and flavor.

WHEN: Cocktail party, casual drinks with friends, an easy predinner snack.

WHY: Because they're beautiful and dramatic, and it's fun saying, "Here. Have a goat cheese ball."

I loved goat cheese back when it wasn't cool to love goat cheese. I don't know when that time was, or if it ever even existed, but all I know is that I've loved goat cheese longer than I've been alive. That makes zero sense, but so would a life without goat cheese. It's so sharp yet mild, crumbly yet creamy, and it's such a versatile ingredient, whether you're making pizza, pasta, or appetizers. This is an elegant way to work goat cheese into any gathering. The possibilities for coatings are endless, and can be tailored to suit whatever occasion, from casual to fancy.

16 ounces plain goat cheese

¼ cup sour cream

½ teaspoon kosher salt

¼ cup sesame seeds, toasted (see Note, page 80)

¼ cup minced dill

2 tablespoons finely chopped dried cherries

2 tablespoons finely chopped walnuts

Pop-in-your-mouth perfection!

1. In a food processor, combine the goat cheese, sour cream, and salt.

2. Process until smooth, about 30 seconds.

3. Scoop the mixture into 24 (or so) 1-tablespoon portions and place them on a parchment-lined sheet pan.

4. Transfer to the freezer to firm slightly, about 15 minutes.

5. Use your hands to roll the goat cheese into neat balls. Set them aside.

6. Place the sesame seeds and dill in separate small bowls. In a third bowl, mix together the dried cherries and walnuts.

7. One at a time, drop 8 of the goat cheese balls into the sesame seeds and roll around to coat.

8. Coat another 8 in the dill . . .

9. And the remaining 8 in the cherry/nut mixture.

10. Place them on the sheet pan (you can see I'm partial to dill!), then cover them with plastic wrap and keep in the fridge. Transfer to a platter just before serving.

Variations

» *Coat with a mix of chopped fresh herbs— whatever you like!*

» *Coat with chopped sun-dried tomatoes mixed with minced fresh basil.*

» *Any combination of nuts is delicious!*

SMOKED SALMON-CUCUMBER BITES

MAKES ABOUT 16 BITES

WHAT: Lovely little party bites made from cucumber, salmon, and sour cream.

WHEN: Any time you're having guests over and you want to feel a little fancy!

WHY: Because they're as pretty as they are tasty (and they're on the lower-carb side).

I think party bites are my favorite food group, because you can enjoy such a mix of colors, textures, and flavors. These cucumber-salmon bites are so utterly delightful, with a zesty sour cream layer in the center, fresh dill, and a sprinkle of seasoning that's reminiscent of an everything bagel. Get all the elements ready ahead of time and assemble them right before your get-together. They're a cinch to make!

2 teaspoons sesame seeds, toasted (see Note, page 80)

2 teaspoons poppy seeds

1 teaspoon dried minced onion

1 teaspoon dried minced garlic

½ teaspoon coarsely ground black pepper

1½ teaspoons flaky sea salt

¼ cup sour cream

1 tablespoon minced dill, plus little sprigs for garnish

Zest of 1 lemon

1 long, skinny English cucumber

One 4-ounce package sliced smoked salmon, cut into 16 strips

1. In a small bowl, combine the sesame seeds, poppy seeds, onion, garlic, pepper, and ½ teaspoon of the sea salt.

3. In another bowl, combine the sour cream, dill, lemon zest, and remaining 1 teaspoon sea salt.

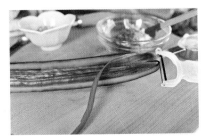

5. With a vegetable peeler, peel alternating strips from the full length of the cucumber.

2. Stir until combined and set aside.

4. Stir until combined and set aside.

6. Use a sharp knife to cut 16 slices of cucumber on a diagonal.

7. To assemble, spoon a dollop of the sour cream mixture on a slice of cucumber.

8. Fold or roll a strip of salmon and place it on the sour cream . . .

9. And, finally, sprinkle on some of the seasoning mix!

10. Arrange the cucumber bites on a platter and garnish them with dill sprigs. So lovely!

One word: Life-changing.
(Or is that two words?)

NOT KNOTS

MAKES 24 TO 26 KNOTS

WHAT: Light, crisp balls of fried dough, man.

WHEN: Game night on TV, appetizer before an Italian dinner, any party!

WHY: Because they're light, crisp balls of fried dough, man.

This is, without a doubt, the most popular item offered on the menu of our pizza joint, P-Town Pizza . . . and it's not even pizza! They're Not Knots, and we named them that because even though they resemble garlic knots, they're not actually knots, hence the name. It's like when I named our new kitty "Kitty Kitty." I'm just not a very complex thinker, I guess. I call things as I see them. And as is the case with any food that is this unbelievably sublime, you can't believe you've lived all the years you have without experiencing it. It doesn't really matter what you call them; they're absolutely some of the most amazing little bites you'll ever pop in your mouth. And they're not even knots—go figure!

1 teaspoon instant or active dry yeast

1½ cups warm water (between 105 and 110°F)

4 cups all-purpose flour

1 teaspoon kosher salt

⅓ cup olive oil, plus more as needed

1 cup (2 sticks) salted butter

10 garlic cloves, finely minced

½ cup freshly grated Parmesan cheese, plus more for serving

About 1 quart vegetable oil, for deep-frying

Warm marinara sauce, for serving

Minced parsley, for serving

1. Sprinkle the yeast over the warm water in a small bowl. Let stand for 5 minutes without stirring.

2. In the bowl of a stand mixer fitted with the paddle attachment, combine the flour and salt . . .

3. Then turn the mixer on low and pour in the olive oil. Let it mix into the flour.

4. Pour in the yeast-water mixture . . .

5. And continue to mix until the dough comes together in a sticky mass.

6. Pour a little olive oil into a large bowl . . .

7. Then form the dough into a rough ball and toss it in the oil to coat the surface.

8. Cover the bowl with a towel and set it in a draft-free place to rise at room temperature until doubled, about 2 hours. Or store in the fridge until you need it, up to 4 days ahead. (It will slowly rise in the fridge; punch it down if you need to!) Bring the refrigerated dough to room temperature before using.

9. When you're ready to make the Not Knots, oil a sheet pan, lay plastic wrap on it, and oil the plastic wrap. Pinch off balls of the dough about 1 inch in diameter.

10. Roll them in your hands to form balls, then place the balls on the prepared sheet pan. Lay another sheet of plastic on top.

11. Set them aside to rise for 2 hours, then gently remove the plastic wrap. They will be very soft and poufy!

12. In a small saucepan, melt the butter with the garlic over medium heat for a couple of minutes to release the flavor, but without letting the garlic brown. Remove from the heat.

13. When you're ready to fry the Not Knots, pour the garlic butter into a large bowl. Stir in the Parmesan.

14. Pour 3 inches vegetable oil into a large Dutch oven and heat over medium-high heat until a deep-frying thermometer registers 350°F. Use a spider or slotted metal spoon to lower 5 or 6 knots into the oil.

15. Turn and push them around in the oil until they are evenly browned and cooked through. They should take only 2 to 2½ minutes to fry.

16. Remove them from the oil, let them drain just briefly, then quickly transfer them to the bowl of garlic-Parmesan butter. Toss to coat completely. They should be buttery, garlicky, and messy! Remove them to a serving plate and fry the rest of the Not Knots in batches, tossing them in the garlic butter as you go.

17. Serve them with a bowl of warm marinara sauce. Sprinkle on some fresh Parmesan and parsley.

Variations

» *Omit the garlic butter and toss in cinnamon sugar for sweet Not Knots!*

» *Toss in powdered sugar.*

» *Leave plain and serve with Nutella.*

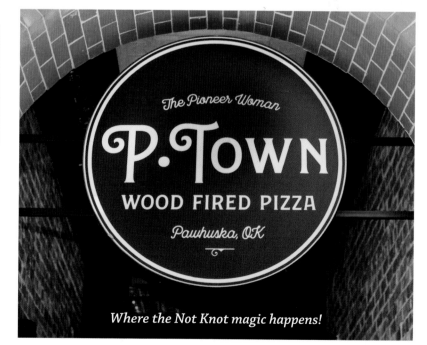

The Pioneer Woman

P.TOWN

WOOD FIRED PIZZA

Pawhuska, OK

Where the Not Knot magic happens!

TACO-STUFFED MINI PEPPERS

MAKES ABOUT 40 MINI PEPPERS

WHAT: Sweet mini peppers stuffed with taco meat and topped with fixins.

WHEN: Any party, any time!

WHY: They're low-carb, they're colorful, and they're packed with flavor.

I've made these colorful little appetizers time and time again because they're bright and pretty, while also being meaty and hearty, while also being low-carb and luscious. I love this world we live in! If you're making these for a party, you can whip up the meat mixture and halve and seed the peppers ahead of time. Then all you have to do right before guests show up at your house is whip up the avocado crema, reheat the meat mixture, and assemble the heck out of these babies. They're super tasty!

2 tablespoons olive oil

1 medium yellow onion, diced

2 garlic cloves, minced

1½ pounds ground beef

2 tablespoons chili powder

1 teaspoon ground cumin

Pinch of cayenne pepper

Kosher salt and black pepper

2 tablespoons tomato paste

1 small avocado, pitted and peeled

¼ cup sour cream

Zest and juice of 1 lime

2 tablespoons whole milk

One 16-ounce bag mini sweet peppers, halved lengthwise (not stemmed) and seeded

6 ounces crumbled queso fresco, for serving

1 cup cilantro leaves, for serving

1. In a large skillet, heat the olive oil over medium-high heat. Add the onion and garlic and sauté for about 4 minutes, until the onion begins to soften.

2. Add the beef and season with the chili powder, cumin, cayenne, 1 teaspoon salt, and ½ teaspoon black pepper.

3. Cook the meat, breaking it up as needed, until completely cooked through, about 5 minutes, then drain the excess grease. Add the tomato paste . . .

4. And stir it in and cook for 2 minutes.

5. Pour in ¾ cup water, then simmer for 10 minutes, stirring as needed. Taste and adjust the seasoning.

6. Meanwhile, make the avocado crema: In a small bowl, mash the avocado with a fork until mostly smooth.

7. Add the sour cream, lime zest, lime juice, and a pinch of salt. Stir to combine . . .

8. Then add the milk . . .

9. And stir to combine. Because of the avocado, you'll want to make this right before serving!

10. Scoop the meat mixture into the halved peppers . . .

11. Then top with queso fresco and a drizzle of the avocado crema . . .

12. Add cilantro leaves, then finish the rest! Serve immediately.

CHUCK'S SHRIMP BROCHETTES

MAKES 12 BROCHETTES

WHAT: Giant shrimp stuffed with jalapeños and cheese, then wrapped in bacon and grilled.

WHEN: A summer barbecue, a winter party, game day, any day!

WHY: Because when it comes to delicious appetizers, my father-in-law knows what's up, man.

My father-in-law, Chuck, is such a great eater. Food is very import-ant to him, and my late mother-in-law, Nan, used to joke (though she wasn't joking) that as soon as Chuck finished a meal, he'd start planning what his next one was going to be. One of his all-time favorite foods is these bacon-wrapped shrimp skewers, which he enjoys at a Mexican restaurant in Fort Worth, Texas. Those skewers are always served with melted butter and pico de gallo on the side, and I wanted to master them in case the roads from Oklahoma to Texas are ever closed and Chuck can't get to them. It's always good to be prepared!

12 extra-jumbo (13/15 count) shrimp, peeled and deveined, tails on

¼ cup crumbled queso fresco or Cotija cheese

1 large jalapeño, partially seeded (to control the heat) and finely minced

6 thin slices bacon, halved crosswise

Vegetable oil, for the pan

8 tablespoons (1 stick) salted butter

1 large tomato, finely diced

½ yellow onion, finely diced

¼ cup chopped cilantro

Juice of 1 lime

Kosher salt and black pepper

Cameron, Tim, and Ladd bringing in the cows.

1. Make a deep slit along the back of each shrimp. Stuff each with some queso fresco and a little jalapeño. (Set aside half of the jalapeño for the pico de gallo.)

4. Melt 4 tablespoons (½ stick) of the butter and brush it on the shrimp.

7. Set aside to cool slightly, then remove and discard the toothpicks.

2. Wrap the shrimp with a half-piece of bacon to hold the ingredients inside the shrimp. Secure with a toothpick. Repeat with the rest of the shrimp and bacon.

5. Turn them over and baste them frequently . . .

8. To make the pico de gallo, in a medium bowl, combine the tomato, onion, cilantro, the reserved jalapeño, the lime juice, and salt and black pepper to taste.

3. Heat a grill pan over medium heat. Oil the pan and lay on the shrimp.

6. Grilling until the bacon is cooked and the shrimp are opaque.

9. Melt the remaining 4 tablespoons butter in a clean dish. Serve the shrimp on a platter with the melted butter and the pico de gallo.

QUESO FUNDIDO

MAKES ABOUT 4 CUPS

WHAT: The queso dip of all queso dips. Meaty, spicy, cheesy, amen.

WHEN: Big game, Saturday night movie, party food!

WHY: It's basically melted cheese in a skillet with peppers and sausage. Case closed.

Queso dip is a religion in this part of the country, but it's usually in the form of "velvety" processed cheese and Ro*Tel—a mix of diced tomatoes and green chiles. I'll eat that queso any day of the week and twice on Sundays, but if you put *this* queso fundido in front of me, I'll forsake every other queso that came before it. This is, quite literally, *queso* in its most literal translation: a big ol' skillet of melted cheese. Oh, sure, I throw in some peppers and sausage just for appearances, because it would be embarrassing if someone saw me melting nothing but cheese in a skillet and devouring it, right?

Okay, friends. No more talking. You have to go make this now! You can eat it with chips, or you can take the healthier route and serve it with carrot sticks and cauliflower florets. It is absolutely dreamy!

The greatest queso dip!

1 tablespoon olive oil

4 ounces Mexican chorizo

1 small onion, finely diced

1 green bell pepper, seeded and finely diced

1 yellow bell pepper, seeded and finely diced

¼ cup tequila (optional)

1 pound Monterey Jack cheese, grated

8 ounces white Cheddar cheese, grated

Chili powder

2 Roma tomatoes, finely diced

Kosher salt

¼ cup chopped cilantro leaves, for serving

Tortilla chips, for serving

Carrot sticks and cauliflower florets, for serving

1. Preheat the oven to 400°F.

2. In a 9-inch cast-iron skillet, heat the olive oil over medium heat. Add the chorizo and cook, crumbling it as you go, until browned and cooked through.

4. Without cleaning the skillet, add the onion and bell peppers.

6. Mix the cheeses together, then cover the bottom of a medium ovenproof skillet with one-third of the cheese mixture . . .

3. Remove the chorizo from the skillet and drain it on paper towels (chorizo is very greasy!). Pour off any excess fat from the skillet.

5. Cook the veggies over medium-high heat, stirring frequently, until they brown and soften, about 5 minutes. Turn off the heat and stir in the tequila, if using. Turn the heat back on to medium-high and cook until the vegetables are golden brown and the liquor has reduced, 2 to 3 minutes more. Remove the vegetables from the skillet and set them aside. Turn off the heat.

7. Add one-third of the vegetables . . .

8. And one-third of the chorizo.

9. Continue with two more layers, ending with chorizo. Sprinkle the top with chili powder.

10. Bake until the cheese is totally melted, hot, and slightly bubbling around the edges, 4 to 5 minutes. Watch it constantly, as you don't want the cheese to get overly melted and hard. But you want it to be sizzling!

11. Top with the tomatoes, a sprinkle of kosher salt, and the cilantro.

12. Serve immediately with tortilla chips . . .

13. Or carrot sticks and cauliflower florets if you want to avoid chips!

Variations

» *Use any combination of melting cheeses you'd like.*
» *Add chopped mushrooms to the onion-pepper mixture.*
» *Use pork breakfast sausage instead of chorizo for a milder flavor.*

Girl bosses! (Just ask their brothers . . .)

HEAVENLY STUFFED MUSHROOMS

MAKES 24 MUSHROOMS

WHAT: Exceedingly flavorful mushrooms stuffed with sausage, cheese, and love.

WHEN: Cocktail party, wine with friends, or (if you just eat a few with a salad) a light dinner.

WHY: Because stuffed mushrooms never get old. (I've eaten them for over forty years, man; I should know.)

Stuffed mushrooms. What is there to say? I've loved them since I was a little girl, and I've never once gotten tired of them. There are so many possibilities for stuffing them with delicious ingredients, from spinach to onions to various cheeses . . . I just adore them. And I especially love this version, which has all the glorious flavors you'd expect, with the addition of a big, melty base of cheese in each 'shroom. They're a dream! They're from Heaven. (Hence the name.)

24 white button mushrooms

8 ounces Fontina cheese, cut into 24 cubes

½ pound Italian sausage

½ yellow onion, finely diced

4 garlic cloves, minced

1 tablespoon fresh oregano leaves, minced

1 tablespoon fresh thyme leaves, minced

1 tablespoon minced parsley, plus more for garnish

⅓ cup white wine

1½ cups panko breadcrumbs

1. Preheat the oven to 350°F.

2. Pull the stems out of the mushrooms. Set the stems aside.

4. Chop the stems finely and set them aside.

6. Add the onion, garlic, and chopped mushroom stems. Stir and cook for 3 minutes, until the sausage is browned. Drain off any excess grease.

3. Place the mushrooms on a sheet pan and stick a cube of the cheese snugly inside each one.

5. In a large skillet, crumble and begin to cook the sausage over medium-high heat.

7. Add the minced herbs . . .

8. And stir to combine, then pour in the wine . . .

11. And stir to combine.

13. And repeat with the rest. Bake until the topping is deep golden brown, about 20 minutes.

9. And stir and cook for 3 minutes, until the wine has almost fully cooked off.

12. Use a tablespoon scoop to mound the mixture on top of a mushroom . . .

14. Transfer to a serving platter, sprinkle with more parsley, and serve.

10. Turn off the heat and add the panko . . .

Variation

» *Substitute crushed pork rinds for the panko breadcrumbs for a lower-carb stuffed mushroom.*

» *Substitute Brie or Camembert for the Fontina.*

MAKE A SLEW!

Stuffed mushrooms aren't necessarily a quick appetizer to pull together at the last minute, so if I'm going to go to the trouble of preparing a batch, I often just go ahead and double (and yes, sometimes triple or more!) the recipe, then store the bounty in the freezer. Here's how to freeze and reheat: Stuff the mushrooms, then place them on a sheet pan in the freezer for 45 minutes to flash freeze. After that, you can place them in a single layer in freezer bags or container, sealing them as tight as you can. Store them flat in the freezer, and when you need them later, just bake them according to the recipe directions, adding 15 to 18 minutes to the time. When my sister is visiting or a friend drops by, I'm always glad to have an easy appetizer to pop in the oven—and a tasty one at that. Stuffed mushrooms are freezer stars!

SPICY PIGS IN A BLANKET

MAKES 16 CUTE LITTLE PIGS

WHAT: Cute (and strangely elegant) sausages wrapped in puff pastry.

WHEN: Cocktail parties, casual gatherings, game night, movie night.

WHY: Because the irony of sophisticated puff pastry wrapped around silly little cocktail wieners will make you laugh. (And then you'll taste them and fall in love!)

I love a good ol' pig in a blanket. I don't care what the pig is and I don't care what the blanket is. Of course, I (along with most Middle Americans) grew up with little sausages wrapped in canned crescent dough or biscuits, and I'll pop those in my mouth any day of the week if they're put in front of me. But ohhh . . . how a sheet of puff pastry elevates the little cuties to new levels! I like to add a little slice of jalapeño and cheese to make them even more delectable, but I'm ornery that way. (Come be ornery with me!)

1 sheet frozen puff pastry, thawed	2 slices pepper Jack cheese, each cut into 8 pieces	4 tablespoons (½ stick) butter, melted, for brushing
16 miniature cocktail sausages	16 jarred pickled jalapeño slices	Whole-grain mustard, for serving

1. Preheat the oven to 375°F.

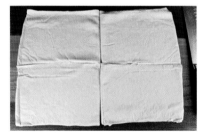

2. Lay the puff pastry sheet flat, and cut it into four equal pieces . . .

4. Cut a slit across the top of a sausage . . .

6. Roll it up snug. So cute!

3. Then cut each piece into four strips.

5. Then fill it with a piece of cheese, lay a jalapeño slice on top, and place it at the end of one of the puff pastry strips.

7. Lay it on a sheet pan and repeat to make the rest!

8. Brush the tops with melted butter . . .

9. And bake until golden brown, 20 to 22 minutes.

10. Let them cool slightly, then serve them with whole-grain mustard.

Josh and Snort.
(Best horse name ever!)

Drinks

Wine has always been my adult beverage of choice, but in the past year, I have learned to really appreciate the loveliness of a single delicious cocktail. These are some of my favorites, most of them hailing from my pizza restaurant in our small town. They're all about the flavor, so they invite very slow sipping and savoring. (That they also happen to be pretty is another plus!) These are perfect for a night with your sweetie or a gathering of friends. (Psst. I've included some mocktail variations if you prefer no alcohol!)

This one's nonalcoholic!

SPICY COWGIRL

MAKES 1 GENEROUS DRINK (WHICH 2 CAN SHARE!)

WHAT: The most irresistible iced coffee you will ever taste. Slightly spicy and very nicey.

WHEN: Any morning you need a little charge, any afternoon you need a little pick-me-up, or any evening you need a bit of spicy coffee sweetness.

WHY: It's the best-selling coffee drink at The Mercantile for a reason. Truly magical!

First, let me get this out of the way: Iced coffee is my life. It's how I start each day, it's something I think about several times a day, and it's basically a religion for me at this point. This iced-coffee-on-steroids drink was created as a signature offering at my restaurant in our town, and it very quickly (within the first 24 hours) became the best-selling drink on the coffee menu. It's an irresistible combination of coffee, cream, vanilla, spice, and chocolate that ticks all the boxes, and I actually have to limit myself to one a week to avoid being sucked too deeply into the whirlwind of bliss. And the whirlwind of my jeans no longer fitting.

SPICY SYRUP
(MAKES ABOUT 1½ CUPS)

1 cup sugar

1 serrano or jalapeño, sliced

FRENCH PRESS COLD BREW
(MAKES ABOUT 4 CUPS)

½ cup ground dark roast coffee

TO MAKE 1 LARGE DRINK

¼ cup heavy cream

2 tablespoons vanilla syrup

¾ cup cold brew coffee

½ cup whole milk

1 tablespoon spicy syrup

1 tablespoon chocolate sauce

Ice

Dash of ground cinnamon

Dash of cayenne pepper

1. Up to a week in advance, make the spicy syrup: In a small saucepan, combine the sugar and 1 cup water and stir to dissolve the sugar.

2. Add the pepper slices and bring the sugar water to a simmer over medium heat. Remove from the heat and let cool completely . . .

3. Then pour the syrup into a small jar, put on the lid, and store in the fridge until you need it.

4. You can also make the French press cold brew up to a week in advance: Add the coffee to a French press. (Note: If you don't have a French press, you can steep the coffee in a regular pitcher.)

7. Then place the lid on with the plunger up. Steep in the fridge for at least 12 hours.

8. After the coffee has steeped, slowly push down the plunger to strain it. (If using a regular pitcher, strain it through cheesecloth!)

5. Pour in cold water to the fill line (it should be about 4 cups).

6. Stir gently to mix . . .

Spicy Cowgirls are the best!

9. When you're ready to make the Spicy Cowgirl, combine the cream with the vanilla syrup.

10. Whisk vigorously until soft peaks form, about 2 minutes.

11. To a jar or cocktail shaker, add ¾ cup of the cold brew . . .

12. And the milk.

13. Retrieve 1 tablespoon of the spicy syrup . . .

14. And add it to the jar or shaker.

15. Add the chocolate sauce, then tighten the lid on the jar or shaker . . .

16. And shake the heck out of it for 1 minute, until the milk is frothed.

17. Fill a glass with ice and pour in the mixture, leaving a little room at the top.

18. Spoon on a good layer of the vanilla cream . . .

19. And sprinkle on the cinnamon and cayenne. Your life is about to change!

Variations

» *To save some steps, use store-bought cold brew coffee and/or store-bought spicy syrup.*

» *If you can't find spicy syrup, simply use simple syrup and add a dash of cayenne to the jar with the rest of the drink ingredients.*

MARGA-REE-TA

MAKES 1 MARGARITA

WHAT: An herbalicious, cucumberlicious margarita on the rocks.

WHEN: After five o'clock!

WHY: Because the herbs give it an unexpected kick of flavor that'll change yer margarita life forever.

I've never been a huge fan of margaritas, but this version created by P-Town mixologists changed all of that. It contains not just the standard lemon-lime flavor, but also a knock-your-socks-off kick of deliciousness from cilantro, mint, and (are you ready?) cucumber. The first time I took a sip, I felt like I was coming home. Or I felt like home had come to me. Or I felt happy that there were actually things inside the margarita that I could eat. The best of both worlds!

1 lime wedge

Kosher salt, for the rim

A few cilantro leaves

2 fresh mint leaves, plus a mint sprig for garnish

7 thin cucumber slices

2 ounces tequila (I used Avion)

½ ounce vodka (I used Grey Goose)

2 ounces simple syrup (see Note, page 133)

1 ounce fresh lime juice

1 ounce fresh lemon juice

Ice

1. First, prepare the glass: Run a lime wedge all around the edge of a mason jar . . .

3. Set the glass aside.

5. The mint leaves . . .

2. And dip it in a dish of salt.

4. Fill a cocktail shaker with ice, then add the cilantro . . .

6. And 3 of the cucumber slices.

7. Pour in the tequila and vodka.

10. Next, add the simple syrup, lime juice, and lemon juice.

13. Then strain the drink into the jar . . .

8. Use a muddler to mash everything together . . .

11. Vigorously shake the cocktail shaker for a good 10 seconds.

14. And top with a pretty sprig of mint. Enjoy!

9. Until the herbs are broken up and the full force of their flavors has been released!

12. Fill the rimmed jar with ice and arrange the remaining 4 cucumber slices along the inside of the jar . . .

Nonalcoholic Variation

» *Replace the tequila, vodka, and lemon juice with lemonade!*

BERRYLICIOUS!

I love having fruit purees on standby to spike my margaritas (or Marga-REE-tas!). For a simple strawberry version, combine 2 pints hulled strawberries, ½ cup sugar, and the juice of 2 limes in a blender. Puree thoroughly, then store in a jar in the fridge. Add a healthy splash to your margaritas after they're mixed and give them a gentle stir. Fruity and fantastic!

CAPRESE BLOODY MARY

MAKES 1 GENEROUS BLOODY MARY (AND ENOUGH MIX FOR 8 DRINKS)

WHAT: A zesty tomato cocktail that's as much appetizer as drink.

WHEN: Friday night with friends, Sunday brunch with . . . friends!

WHY: Because it's a showstopper in a glass!

It took me years and years to love a Bloody Mary. I won't tell you how many years, but I will tell you that it just happened last summer, when I first tasted this mash-up of a Bloody Mary and a Caprese salad. If one can fall in love with a tomato-based cocktail, well, it happened to me. A hit in every way! The garnish is lovely, the whole drink is totally gorgeous, and the base mix is loaded with amazing flavor. It took me a while to see the Bloody Mary light . . . but better late than never!

1. Make the Bloody Mary mix: In a blender, combine the tomato puree and tomato juice . . .

3. Add the Worcestershire, salt, pepper, celery salt, garlic, and Tabasco . . .

2. Along with the lime juice.

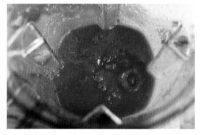

4. And blend until everything is combined. Pour into a jar and chill completely in the fridge.

BLOODY MARY MIX (MAKES ABOUT 4 CUPS)

One 28-ounce can good-quality tomato puree

1 cup tomato juice

Juice of 1 lime

1 tablespoon Worcestershire sauce

1 teaspoon kosher salt

1 teaspoon black pepper

1 teaspoon celery salt

1 teaspoon granulated garlic

½ teaspoon Tabasco sauce

TO MAKE 1 DRINK

1 tablespoon balsamic glaze, plus more for drizzling

Ice

4 ounces Bloody Mary mix

2½ ounces vodka

2 cherry or grape tomatoes, halved

1 ounce fresh mozzarella, cut into small cubes

1 fresh basil leaf

*A drink that's
more like a dinner!*

5. When you're ready to make the drink, place the balsamic glaze in a small shallow dish and dip in the rim of a large glass.

6. Let the excess drip off, then set the glass aside.

7. Place a little ice in a cocktail shaker and add the Bloody Mary mix and vodka. Shake to your heart's content . . .

8. Then fill the glass with ice and strain in the Bloody Mary!

9. Make a skewer by threading the tomato halves and mozzarella cubes on a party toothpick, then lay it across the top of the glass. Stick a basil leaf out of the top of the drink.

10. Drizzle more glaze all over the top. Slurpalicious!

Nonalcoholic Variation

» **Substitute soda water or seltzer for the vodka.**

FOUR MORE!

Shrimp Cocktail Bloody Mary
Stir ½ teaspoon prepared horseradish into the cocktail shaker with the rest of the ingredients. Serve the drink in a glass with a cooked colossal shrimp on the rim.

BLT Bloody Mary
Serve the regular Bloody Mary as directed, then stick 2 strips of cooked bacon, 1 celery stalk (with leaves), and 1 wooden skewer of grape tomatoes in the glass.

Berry Bloody Mary
Add 1 tablespoon honey to the cocktail shaker with the other ingredients, place a whole strawberry on the rim of the glass, and sprinkle raspberries, blackberries, and blueberries on top of the drink.

Scary Bloody Mary
Prepare the drink as directed and garnish with a skewer of anything you can get your hands on: olives, cubes of salami, meatballs, cubes of cheese, pickles. (I've even seen mini burgers and Buffalo wings!)

BUTTERFLY MARTINI

MAKES 1 MARTINI

WHAT: A mysteriously floral cocktail that tastes as pretty as it looks.

WHEN: Girls' night in, or any time you need a super-special libation.

WHY: Because the combination of liqueurs and syrups results in a taste experience that cannot be believed.

I have found the cocktail of my dreams, and I only had to open a pizza joint in our small town to do it. (No biggie! Ha.) At P-Town Pizza, I'm lucky to have a young, hip staff, and this cocktail was one of their creations when we opened our doors. I'm not a big cocktail drinker, but this drink is absolutely my kryptonite. The flavors are everything I want in life, and I knew at first sip that the two of us would live a long and happy life together. Just as long as I have only one per month.

Ice

1 ounce elderflower liqueur
(such as St-Germain)

2 ounces Bombay Sapphire gin

½ ounce crème de violette
liqueur

½ ounce hibiscus rose syrup
(or plain rose syrup)

½ ounce simple syrup
(see Note, page 133)

1 edible flower (I used a
Karma orchid—ask your produce
manager!)

1. Fill a cocktail shaker with ice . . .

3. The crème de violette . . .

5. Place the lid on the shaker and shake for 30 seconds. Strain into a small glass . . .

2. Then add the elderflower liqueur and gin . . .

4. And both syrups.

6. And place the flower on top. Pretty, pretty!

THE HOMESCHOOLER

MAKES 1 DRINK

WHAT: Exactly! WHAT?!? Homeschoolers aren't supposed to have any fun!

WHEN: When you want to have a little fun.

WHY: Because candy and cocktails are sometimes a cool little combo. (Adults only, please!)

This cheeky-as-heck cocktail is a nod to all the "Smartie" homeschoolers out there who spend their days quizzing their offspring on Latin declensions and reciting the *Iliad* in their pajamas. It's a sweet-tart little cocktail with a citrusy-apricot zip, and it's fun for a room full of friends, whether they homeschool their kids or not! And the bonus prize for a long day of teaching? A classic candy necklace cascading right out of the glass. What's the world coming to? (Hey! Great question for philosophy class!)

1 tablespoon thick cherry grenadine

1 package Smarties candy, crushed

Ice

1¼ ounces gin (I used Uncle Val's Botanical Gin)

4 ounces apricot brandy

1 ounce orange juice

Candy necklace, for serving

1. Pour the grenadine into a small, shallow dish and dip in the rim of a martini glass to make it extra sticky.

3. Set the glass aside while you make the drink.

5. And the orange juice.

2. Place the crushed Smarties in a separate dish and dip the rim into the candy to coat.

4. Fill a cocktail shaker with ice, then add the gin and brandy . . .

6. Shake the drink until it's very cold, then strain it into the glass. Plunk in a candy necklace. Party time!

Replace the booze with pineapple juice for a nonalcoholic version!

OKLAHOMA PRAIRIE FIRE

MAKES 1 DRINK

WHAT: A sweet-tart citrus drink with a hint of smoke!

WHEN: When the temperature outside is risin'.

WHY: The color of the blood orange juice makes this cocktail vivid and stunning.

Before I first tasted this drink, I hadn't had a lot of experience with mezcal, a kind of alcohol that is sometimes mistaken for tequila, since both are made from the agave plant. Mezcal is a different spirit altogether, bringing a distinctive smoky flavor to any drink. This cocktail celebrates the intense red-orange of an Oklahoma prairie fire (hopefully a controlled one!) as well as the smoke that rises from our part of the country in March and April every year—and it's one of the most refreshing adult beverages you'll ever try.

¼ teaspoon ancho chile powder

½ teaspoon table salt

Lime wedge

Ice

2 ounces mezcal or tequila

2 ounces blood orange juice or regular orange juice

Juice of 1 large lime

1 ounce simple syrup (see Note, page 133)

½ ounce grenadine

6 dashes of orange bitters

1. To prepare the glass, mix the chile powder and salt in a small dish.

3. Then dip the rim of the glass in the chile salt . . .

5. Fill a cocktail shaker with ½ cup ice, then add the mezcal . . .

2. Run a lime wedge around the rim of a zombie glass (or Collins glass) . . .

4. Until it has a nice smoky-salty coating. Fill the glass two-thirds full with ice and set it aside.

6. Blood orange juice . . .

7. Lime juice . . .

9. Grenadine . . .

11. Then strain the drink into the glass.

8. Simple syrup . . .

10. And bitters. Place the lid on the shaker and shake it for 20 seconds . . .

12. Serve right away!

Note: To make simple syrup, combine 1 cup sugar and 1 cup water in a small saucepan and boil until the sugar is dissolved and the mixture becomes a syrup. Store in the fridge.

Nonalcoholic Variation

» *Prepare the glass as opposite. Shake together ⅓ cup blood orange juice, the juice of 1 lime, 2 tablespoons simple syrup, and 2 tablespoons grenadine. Pour over ice, then top with sparkling water or sparkling lemonade.*

SPIKED SPA WATER

MAKES 1 DRINK

WHAT: A lower-carb, spa-inspired cocktail.

WHEN: When you want to have a few sips of an adult beverage without all the calories.

WHY: Because no matter the occasion, the cucumber flavor will make you feel zen.

What I love most about our cocktails at P-Town Pizza is that there is so much variety that there's always a drink to suit anyone's fancy. While I love the more indulgent cocktails on the menu, there are just those occasions when I'm grateful for this absolute delight of a cocktail. The cucumber in the drink serves three distinct purposes: One, it makes the glass look pretty. Two, it adds amazing spa-like flavor to the drink. Three, it incorporates a little snack component to the cocktail; just eat the cucumber slices when the drink is gone. Score! A direct hit. You'll love this drink.

½ cucumber

Ice

1 ounce cucumber-infused vodka

Juice of ½ lime

Splash of sparkling water

Lime wheel, for garnish

1. Slice the cucumber as thinly as you can. At P-Town, we use a mandoline, but if you can accomplish it with a knife, great! You should wind up with about 10 very thin slices.

2. Lay the cucumber slices around the inside of a martini-shaped (or similar) glass. Depending on the shape of the glass, you can do two rows of cucumbers, if desired.

3. Fill the glass with ice to anchor the cucumber slices. Set the glass aside.

4. Place 1 cup of ice in a cocktail shaker, then pour in the cucumber vodka . . .

5. And squeeze in the lime juice. This is such a fantastically fresh drink!

6. Shake vigorously for 10 seconds, then strain the drink into the glass.

7. Top off with enough sparkling water to fill the glass.

8. Add a lime wheel to the edge of the glass and enjoy. And be sure to eat the cucumbers!

Nonalcoholic Variation

» **Keep that cocktail shaker in the cabinet! Just squeeze the juice of a whole lime straight into the cucumber-lined, ice-filled glass, then top off with sparkling water and garnish with lime.**

Walter.
He's a
good egg.

Chicken

Can we just talk about how voluminously versatile chicken is? The white stuff highlights the flavors you cook it in, the dark stuff stands proud in its inherent deliciousness, and the whole family's happy no matter which direction you go. The recipes in this chapter use different parts of the chicken, from tenders to thighs to the whole durn burd. Hooray for chicken!

PORK RIND CHICKEN STRIPS

MAKES 2 SERVINGS

WHAT: Crispy fried chicken strips coated in crispy pork rinds.

WHEN: Weeknight dinner (with salad), weekend appetizer, or snack.

WHY: Pork rinds have zero carbs, and they make for a tasty flour alternative for fried chicken.

When I first got wind of the concept of using crushed pork rinds as breading for chicken, I knew immediately that I was equal to the task. Although pork rinds had never been a glamorous snack before the low-carb craze set in (after which they became positively glam), I had always appreciated their porky, salty crunchiness and was excited to try this crazy new idea. Still, I was a little skeptical, if for no other reason than "pork rind chicken strips" sounded so confusing from a barnyard perspective . . . so I was positively elated when my first batch was absolutely amazing: crispy, crunchy, pleasantly salty, flavorful. And with essentially no carbs. Oh my! Try these soon, friends. I know you'll love them. (And the avocado dipping sauce is the perfect complement!)

PORK RIND CHICKEN STRIPS

2 boneless, skinless chicken breasts, cut into thin strips

⅓ cup buttermilk

1 teaspoon hot sauce

Kosher salt and black pepper

One 3-ounce bag of pork rinds

1 large egg, beaten

Vegetable oil, for shallow-frying

AVOCADO DIPPING SAUCE

1 avocado, pitted and peeled

¼ cup mayonnaise

2 tablespoons minced dill

1 garlic clove, pressed

Juice of 1 lime

Kosher salt and black pepper

1. Place the chicken strips in a plastic zipper bag or a bowl, then add the buttermilk, hot sauce, ½ teaspoon salt, and ½ teaspoon pepper.

2. Smush everything together to mix. Place the bag in the fridge to marinate for 30 minutes.

3. Meanwhile, make the avocado dipping sauce: In a food processor combine the avocado, mayo, dill, garlic, lime juice, and a dash each of salt and pepper.

4. Process until smooth, place in a bowl, and refrigerate until needed.

7. In a separate bowl, mix the egg with a dash of salt and pepper.

10. Quickly dunk the strip into the egg . . .

5. Place the pork rinds in a separate zipper bag. Seal the bag . . .

8. One strip at a time, lay the chicken in the pork rinds . . .

11. And then again in the pork rinds, pressing to secure them to the chicken.

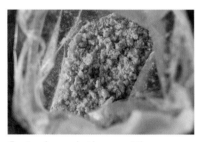

6. And crush them with your hands until mostly broken up with some bigger pieces mixed in. Transfer to a shallow bowl.

9. And turn it over so that the crumbs coat it.

12. Place the strip on a sheet pan and repeat until all the strips are breaded.

13. In a large skillet, heat 1 inch of oil over medium-high heat. Cook the strips in batches until golden brown on both sides and cooked through, about 5 minutes total.

14. Place the strips on a rack over a sheet pan or on a paper towel to drain.

15. Serve them with the avocado dipping sauce!

PORK RIND REVOLUTION

Millennials might not be aware of this, but until recently pork rinds had long been relegated to a small section of the supermarket snack aisle, tragically eclipsed by the trillions of varieties of potato and tortilla chips. But thanks to the low-carb craze that's sweeping the nation (pork rinds have zero carbs), they've made a miraculous and unexpected comeback, and have even been elevated to levels of status and sophistication in some circles. And I love it! (I always root for the underdog.)

Pork rinds are, simply, the rind (or skin) of pork, which is dried and fried, which causes it to puff and become light and crunchy. The rinds have a very mild flavor of their own, but their crispy, porous texture lends itself well to any seasoning mix, much like potato chips do.

Aside from being a tasty no-carb snack, pork rinds also make a great breading (as seen above). But it doesn't stop there! I've seen pork rind nachos, pork rind pizza crust, crumbled pork rinds used as topping for green bean casserole, ground pork rinds stirred into a meatloaf mixture . . . I've even seen them warmed and tossed in cinnamon sugar and dipped in caramel sauce for an easy dessert. Yes, please!

Whether I'm lower-carbing it or (more often) not, I'm sure enjoying this pork rind revolution.

MESQUITE GRILLED CHICKEN

MAKES 4 SERVINGS

WHAT: Incredibly flavorful, smoky chicken breasts.

WHEN: When you want a winner of a chicken dinner.

WHY: Because the chicken is amazing on its own, as well as in tacos or quesadillas.

Poor boneless, skinless chicken breasts. They require so much "assistance" to become something wonderful, as they're just so darn lackluster on their own. Enter: this mesquite marinade! The longer you leave chicken breasts swimming in this stuff, the more blown away you'll be by the chicken once it's grilled. I love grilling it alongside vegetables and calling that dinner when I'm trying to keep things (relatively) light, but it is also perfect on salads, in tacos, or with anything that needs grilled chicken. Double the recipe and keep the grilled breasts in the fridge for easy grabbing—you'll be a serial nibbler!

¼ cup olive oil, plus more for grilling

¼ cup balsamic vinegar

¼ cup packed brown sugar

1 teaspoon mesquite-flavored liquid smoke

4 dashes Worcestershire sauce

4 garlic cloves, minced

Zest and juice of 1 lemon

Kosher salt and black pepper

4 boneless, skinless chicken breasts

Miscellaneous sliced veggies (I used bell pepper, zucchini, and summer squash)

1. In a small pitcher or bowl, whisk together the olive oil, vinegar, brown sugar, liquid smoke, Worcestershire, garlic, lemon zest, lemon juice, 2 teaspoons salt, and 1 teaspoon pepper.

3. Seal the bag and smush the chicken and marinade all together. Let the chicken marinate in the fridge for at least 2 hours or up to 18 hours.

5. Grill the chicken until done in the center, 4 to 5 minutes per side. Cook the vegetables to your liking.

2. Place the chicken in a large plastic zipper bag and pour in the marinade.

4. Remove the chicken from the marinade and shake off the excess (discard the marinade). Heat a grill pan over medium heat and drizzle on some olive oil. Place the chicken on the pan. Add the vegetables and sprinkle everything with salt and pepper.

6. Let the chicken rest for 5 minutes, slice it, and serve it with the vegetables and a side salad!

BUFFALO CHICKEN QUESADILLAS

MAKES SIX 8-INCH QUESADILLAS

WHAT: Boneless diced chicken coated in tangy Louisiana hot sauce and grilled inside a cheesy quesadilla. (Uh . . . and served with ranch. Say wha?!)

WHEN: Friday night dinner, watching a big football game on TV, any time teenagers are in the house.

WHY: Because Buffalo wings and quesadillas have cross-pollinated, and it's a moment for celebration!

Anyone who knew me during my gestatin' years knows that quesadillas were the number one food I requested (demanded?) during the most intense days of pregnancy cravings. But what I might not have mentioned is that if quesadillas were first on the list, Buffalo wings were down around four millionth on the list. That is to say, Buffalo wings were among my most ardent pregnancy *aversions,* and I still to this day have a hard time eating them without feeling the baby kick. And not the good kind of kick, either.

My point is that somehow this recipe, a mash-up of the wonderful and the terrible, has turned out to be a big checkmark in the *yes* column for me. My love for quesadillas completely transforms the Buffalo chicken aspect here . . . and, in fact, the tang of the Buffalo sauce brings something to the quesadillas that I sure wish someone had told me about back in 1997. And 1999. And 2002. And 2004.

Pregnancy aversions. A woman never forgets them.

BLUE CHEESE RANCH DRESSING

½ cup mayonnaise

¼ cup buttermilk

¼ cup sour cream

¼ cup whole milk

2 dashes Worcestershire sauce

1 garlic clove, minced

2 tablespoons minced parsley

2 tablespoons minced dill

¼ teaspoon paprika

½ teaspoon kosher salt

½ teaspoon black pepper

¼ cup blue cheese crumbles

QUESADILLAS

8 tablespoons (1 stick) salted butter

2 boneless, skinless chicken breasts, cut into bite-size pieces

Kosher salt and black pepper

2 garlic cloves, minced

2 celery stalks, thinly sliced, plus celery leaves for garnish

2 green onions, thinly sliced

1½ cups Louisiana hot sauce, such as Frank's

2 dashes Worcestershire sauce

12 small (8-inch) flour tortillas

2 cups grated Monterey Jack cheese

¼ cup blue cheese crumbles, plus more for garnish

1. First, make the blue cheese ranch dressing: Combine all the ingredients in a medium bowl . . .

2. And whisk until mixed well. Keep in the fridge until serving.

3. Make the quesadillas: In a large cast-iron skillet, melt 2 tablespoons of the butter over medium-high heat. Add the chicken, season with salt and pepper, and cook for 2 minutes.

7. In a separate skillet over medium-low heat, melt 1 tablespoon of the butter and add one of the tortillas.

10. Cut each quesadilla into 4 wedges. Serve garnished with celery leaves and extra blue cheese crumbles alongside the blue cheese ranch dressing.

4. Add the garlic, celery, and green onions. Continue to cook, stirring, until the chicken is cooked through, 1 to 2 minutes.

8. Sprinkle on ⅓ cup of the Jack cheese, ½ cup of the chicken, and 2 teaspoons of the blue cheese.

THE SECRET

Here's how to make quesadillas perfect every time:

✿ *Small Tortillas*
This ensures that the cheese melts evenly and the wedges are easier to pick up and eat.

✿ *Melty Cheese*
Monterey Jack is great and readily available. But if your supermarket has it, queso Chihuahua is the cat's (?) meow.

5. Add the hot sauce and Worcestershire . . .

9. Top with a second tortilla, and when the cheese has started to melt, about 2 minutes, flip the quesadilla over. Press to stick everything together, then cook until the bottom tortilla is crispy and golden, 1½ to 2 minutes. Remove and repeat with the remaining butter, tortillas, and filling ingredients.

✿ *Butter and More Butter*
The importance of butter in the skillet is underestimated. The tortilla must be golden, buttery, and crisp. Amen.

✿ *Medium-Low Heat*
This ensures that the cheese will melt completely and the tortillas won't burn.

6. Then stir and allow to thicken slightly for a minute or two. Remove from the heat and set aside.

CHICKEN AND DUMPLINGS

MAKES 8 TO 10 SERVINGS

WHAT: Glorious, comforting chicken stew with big, beautiful dumplings.

WHEN: Any family dinner on any cold night!

WHY: Because some dishes never, ever get old.

I'm a lifelong fan of any recipe that begins with cooking a chicken in a pot and throwing in flavorful balls of dough. Except for those years that I was a vegetarian. But even then, I still would have eaten the dumplings. Guys, if you haven't made a pot of chicken and dumplings for a while, you need to restart that area of your life. If you're a youngster and (egads) have never made it or (egads!!) have never eaten it, you owe it to yourself to allow this one classic comfort food indulgence. It will make you smarter!

2 tablespoons salted butter

2 tablespoons olive oil

One 2½- to 3-pound fryer chicken, cut into pieces

½ cup finely diced carrots

½ cup finely diced celery

1 medium yellow onion, finely diced

½ teaspoon ground thyme

¼ teaspoon ground turmeric

Kosher salt and black pepper

6 cups low-sodium chicken broth

½ cup apple cider

1½ cups plus 2 tablespoons all-purpose flour

½ cup standard ground cornmeal

1 heaping tablespoon baking powder

2 cups half-and-half

2 tablespoons minced parsley

1. In a heavy pot, melt the butter over medium-high heat and add the olive oil. Working in two batches, brown the chicken on both sides . . .

2. And set it aside.

3. In the same pot, combine the carrots, celery, and onion.

WORTH IT!

This dish always takes a little more time (and a few more steps) than the average recipe. But it's all about building flavor and savoring the journey!

4. Cook over medium-low heat, stirring often, until softened, 3 to 4 minutes.

5. Add the thyme and turmeric, along with a pinch each of salt and pepper . . .

6. Then stir and cook for 1 minute.

7. Pour in the chicken broth and apple cider and stir to combine.

8. Add the browned chicken and bring the liquid to a boil . . .

9. Then reduce the heat to low, cover the pot, and simmer for 25 minutes.

10. While the chicken is simmering, make the dough for the dumplings: Sift together 1½ cups flour, the cornmeal, baking powder, 1 teaspoon salt, and ½ teaspoon pepper.

11. Add 1½ cups of the half-and-half and stir gently to combine . . .

12. Then add the parsley and stir gently to combine. Set the dough aside while you work on the chicken so the dry ingredients have a chance to absorb the liquid.

13. By now the chicken is done! (And your kitchen smells great.)

14. Remove the chicken from the pot and set it on a sheet pan. Use 2 forks to remove the meat from the bones . . .

15. And continue until all the meat is shredded.

16. Place the chicken back in the pot and stir it in.

17. In a small pitcher, combine the remaining ½ cup half-and-half and 2 tablespoons flour and stir it with a fork.

18. Add it to the pot and stir to combine. Increase the heat to medium and bring to a simmer.

19. Using a small scoop or spoon, drop tablespoons of dumpling dough into the simmering pot . . .

20. Until the surface is covered in dumplings! Cover the pot and simmer for 15 minutes, gently stirring once halfway through.

21. Look at the gorgeousness! Check the seasoning and add salt if needed. Remove from the heat and let sit for 10 minutes before serving.

22. Serve up bowls with plenty of dumplings and chicken in each one!

Seriously tasty!

CHICKEN WITH ROASTED RED PEPPER SAUCE

MAKES 6 SERVINGS

WHAT: Thin grilled chicken breasts topped with a creamy roasted red pepper sauce.

WHEN: Weeknight dinner, weekend dinner, date night, special company.

WHY: Because it's easy, pretty, and oh so tasty!

There are few pantry items that hold as much promise for me as a jar of roasted red peppers. They're just so charred and flavorful, so bright red and gorgeous, so . . . so . . . so easy to crack open and use! Of course, I love to leave them whole or chop them for salads, but my favorite way to use them is to puree them into a creamy sauce. When I'm feeling indulgent, I'll use the sauce for pasta; if I'm trying to walk the lower-carb walk, it's the perfect topping for juicy grilled chicken. You're gonna want to make this once a week!

6 boneless, skinless chicken breasts	1 tablespoon Italian seasoning	2 cups vegetable broth
3 tablespoons olive oil, plus more for grilling	2 tablespoons salted butter	½ cup heavy cream, or more as needed
2½ teaspoons kosher salt	1 medium yellow onion, chopped	½ cup Parmesan cheese shavings, for serving
1½ teaspoons black pepper	3 garlic cloves, minced	2 tablespoons minced parsley, for serving
	One 15.5-ounce jar roasted red peppers, drained and roughly chopped	

1. Place each chicken breast between two sheets of plastic wrap. Pound them to a uniform thickness, about ¼ inch.

2. Place the chicken in a large plastic zipper bag or bowl. Add the olive oil, 2 teaspoons of the salt, 1 teaspoon of the pepper, and the Italian seasoning to the bag . . .

3. And smush everything together. Seal and allow it to marinate while you make the sauce. (You can leave the chicken to marinate in the fridge for up to 18 hours if you prefer to do this step ahead!)

4. In a large skillet, melt the butter over medium-high heat. Add the onion and garlic and sauté until starting to soften, 2 to 3 minutes.

5. Add the roasted red peppers and cook them, stirring, until hot, 2 to 3 minutes.

6. Pour in the broth, the remaining ½ teaspoon salt and ½ teaspoon pepper, and stir.

7. Bring to a boil . . .

8. Splash in the cream . . .

9. And stir to combine. Simmer the mixture for 5 minutes. Taste, adjust the seasonings, and set aside to cool slightly.

10. Carefully transfer the contents of the skillet to a food processor or blender. (If the liquid is still hot, work in batches, taking care not to fill the blender more than half full.) If you have an immersion blender, you can puree it right in the skillet!

11. Puree the pepper mixture until almost totally blended. There should still be some texture to the peppers.

12. Return the sauce to the skillet and keep warm.

13. Remove the chicken from the marinade (discard the marinade). Heat a grill pan over medium-high heat and grill the chicken until cooked through, about 4 minutes per side.

14. Plate the chicken and spoon a generous amount of sauce on top.

15. Top with Parmesan shavings and a sprinkle of parsley! (Caprese salad makes a nice side.)

Variations

» *Serve the sauce-topped chicken over a generous bed of lightly cooked spinach.*

» *Toss cooked pasta in the sauce. But only if you're feeling ornery.*

» *Make a sandwich out of the sauce-topped chicken: Place a piece of chicken and some of the sauce inside a ciabatta or French bread roll.*

Penny for your thoughts, Fred!

SPATCHCOCK CHICKEN

MAKES 8 TO 10 SERVINGS

WHAT: Perfectly roasted spatchcock chicken and veggies.

WHEN: Weeknight dinner, weekend dinner, dinner for company.

WHY: Because it's fun to say, "I'm gonna spatchcock a chicken for dinner tonight!"

Roasted chicken always makes for a scrumptious dinner, but roasting a whole chicken to perfection can present challenges. Often, by the time the center of the bird is done, the outside of the bird is dry and overcooked, and it's a bummer to go to the trouble of roasting a chicken, only to wind up putting some of it back in to finish. Enter: spatchcocking! When you spatchcock a chicken, you perform a little surgery in order to lay the bird flat on the pan, which allows the meat to roast more evenly throughout. The result is incredibly consistent and superbly delicious, especially when you throw some potatoes and veggies into the picture. Spatchcocking will change your life!

2 tablespoons minced parsley

Leaves from 2 thyme sprigs, minced

⅓ cup olive oil

2 lemons

Kosher salt and black pepper

1 whole chicken (4 pounds), patted dry

1 pound small Yukon Gold potatoes, halved

2 zucchini, halved and cut into sticks

1 cup cherry tomatoes

2 garlic cloves, minced

1. Position a rack in the middle of the oven and preheat it to 475°F.

2. In a small bowl, combine the parsley, thyme, olive oil, the juice of 1 lemon, 1 teaspoon salt, and ½ teaspoon pepper . . .

3. Whisk and set the herb-oil mixture aside.

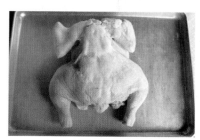

4. To spatchcock the chicken, place the chicken on a sheet pan breast side down.

5. With sharp kitchen shears, cut just along the right side of the backbone, through the skin, meat, and bones . . .

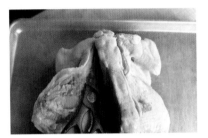

6. Then cut along the left side, too.

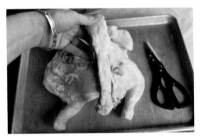

7. Remove the backbone (you can toss it or freeze it to make stock at a later time).

8. Flip the chicken over and lay it flat. With the palm of your hand, press down firmly on the center of the breast. You should hear the breastbone crack!

9. Use your hands to bend the two sides of the breast backward if it needs to crack more.

10. Lay the chicken as flat as it will go . . .

11. And sprinkle the chicken with salt and pepper.

12. In a large bowl, toss the potatoes with 3 tablespoons of the herb-oil mixture.

13. Distribute the potatoes around the chicken and spread 2 tablespoons of the herb-oil mixture on the chicken.

14. Roast for 15 minutes, then reduce the oven temperature to 400°F and continue roasting for 10 minutes.

15. Meanwhile, in a medium bowl, toss together the zucchini, cherry tomatoes, garlic, and the remaining herb-oil mixture.

16. Scatter the veggies around the sheet pan and roast . . .

20. And the two breast halves.

22. Place the potatoes and veggies on a serving platter, then arrange the chicken pieces on top.

17. Until the chicken is totally cooked through, or until an instant-read thermometer inserted into the thick part of the thigh registers 165°F, 12 to 15 minutes. Let the chicken rest for 5 minutes.

21. You just carved a chicken!

23. Squeeze on the juice of the other lemon and serve!

18. Carve off the wings . . .

19. The leg and thigh sections . . .

LEFTOVER CHICKEN: HOW TO USE IT

- ✿ Add to chicken spaghetti casserole.
- ✿ Simmer in enchilada sauce for chicken nachos.
- ✿ Use to make red or green enchiladas.
- ✿ Sprinkle with taco seasoning and add to quesadillas.
- ✿ Make a refreshing chicken salad.
- ✿ Whip up a quick chicken noodle soup.
- ✿ Quick chicken tortilla soup would be even better!
- ✿ Simmer in Louisiana hot sauce and butter and make Buffalo chicken sandwiches.

SLOW COOKER BUTTER CHICKEN

MAKES 6 TO 8 SERVINGS

WHAT: Tender chicken in a buttery tomato sauce with Indian spices.

WHEN: When you want to throw dinner in the slow cooker and fugghetaboutit!

WHY: Because butter chicken is one of the easiest Indian dishes there is, and making it in the slow cooker means it's even easier!

The first time I had butter chicken, I took a bite, closed my eyes, and felt grateful it had entered my life. Butter chicken is a well-loved Indian dish (in my limited American experience, obviously!) originally created as a way of giving new life to dry leftover tandoori chicken! And why is it that the leftover recipes often wind up being even more delicious than the first? This is a slow cooker version, and there's so little fuss to it that when you taste the perfection of the finished product, you'll actually feel guilty over what a cinch it was to make.

One 14-ounce can coconut milk

½ cup heavy cream

3 tablespoons salted butter, cut into pieces

One 14-ounce can stewed tomatoes

2 heaping tablespoons tomato paste

2 tablespoons garam masala (sold in the spice aisle)

5 garlic cloves, minced

1 tablespoon grated fresh ginger

2 tablespoons sriracha sauce

2 pounds boneless, skinless chicken thighs, cut into bite-size pieces

1 large yellow onion, thinly sliced

1 teaspoon kosher salt

½ teaspoon black pepper

Warm naan (Indian flatbread), for serving

Cooked jasmine rice or long-grain rice, for serving

Sour cream or plain Greek yogurt, for serving

Cilantro leaves, for serving

1. Shake the can of coconut milk to mix it up, then pour it into a large pitcher along with the cream and butter . . .

2. Add the stewed tomatoes . . .

3. Then add the tomato paste, garam masala, garlic, ginger, and sriracha. Stir to combine.

4. Combine the chicken and onion in the slow cooker. Sprinkle with the salt and pepper.

5. Pour the sauce over the top . . .

6. Stir to combine . . .

7. Then place the lid on the slow cooker and cook on high for 4 hours or on low for 7 to 8 hours. Stir once in the middle of the cooking process to make sure nothing is sticking to the bottom.

8. Serve a generous helping with naan over a bed of rice . . .

9. Then add a dollop of sour cream and a few cilantro leaves.

Mmmm. Butter chicken! Simply marvelous.

CHICKEN WITH PESTO CREAM SAUCE

MAKES 6 TO 8 SERVINGS

WHAT: Thin, pan-fried chicken breasts topped with pesto cream sauce and served on a bed of greens.

WHEN: Dinner with friends, or any company! It's colorful, pretty, and oh so flavorful.

WHY: Because the pesto cream sauce is good enough to be sipped with a straw. (And the Swiss chard is a lower-carb alternative to pasta or potatoes!)

Pesto cream is a dandy of a sauce because it's as perfect served on sautéed chicken as it is on salmon as it is on sliced medium-rare beef filet. The basil flavor is everywhere, and the cream gives it a richness you won't feel the least bit guilty about because you're serving it with chicken that's sitting *not* on pasta or mashed potatoes, my friends . . . but on deep-green and gorgeous rainbow chard. Ring the bell, sound the drums—cream sauce is here to stay, my chums! (Not that it ever really left . . .)

2 bunches rainbow Swiss chard

1 cup basil leaves

¾ cup freshly grated Parmesan cheese

4 garlic cloves, sliced

3 tablespoons pine nuts

Kosher salt and black pepper

2 tablespoons salted butter

⅓ cup plus 3 tablespoons extra-virgin olive oil

4 boneless, skinless chicken breasts

1 red onion, halved and thinly sliced

Juice of ½ lemon

1½ cups heavy cream

1 cup mixed-color cherry tomatoes, halved

1. Prepare the chard by tearing or cutting the leaves away from the heavy stalks. Discard the stalks.

2. Tear the leaves into pieces and set the chard aside.

3. In a food processor, combine the basil, Parmesan, 1 clove of the garlic, the pine nuts, and a dash of salt.

4. With the machine running, drizzle in ⅓ cup of the olive oil.

5. Taste and adjust the salt as needed. Set the pesto aside.

6. With a sharp knife, carefully slice each chicken breast in half horizontally . . .

9. Remove to a plate and repeat with the remaining cutlets, adding 1 more tablespoon of both butter and olive oil to the pan.

12. And cook, stirring, until lightly wilted, about 2 minutes. Season with salt and pepper.

7. So you have 2 thinner cutlets (for a total of 8). Season the chicken on both sides with salt and pepper.

10. Reduce the heat to medium and add the remaining 1 tablespoon olive oil, the onion, and the remaining garlic. Cook, stirring frequently, until the onion is soft, 4 to 5 minutes.

13. Remove it to a large serving platter (or individual plates) and squeeze the lemon juice over the top.

8. In a large cast-iron skillet, heat 1 tablespoon of the butter and 1 tablespoon of the olive oil over medium-high heat. Add 4 of the chicken cutlets and cook through, 3 to 4 minutes per side.

11. Add the chard . . .

14. Without cleaning the skillet, heat the cream over medium heat for 1 minute. Add ½ cup of the pesto (you can refrigerate any leftover pesto for up to a week).

15. Stir the sauce and return the chicken to the pan, nestling it into the sauce. Bring it to a simmer and let it thicken for about 3 minutes. Taste the sauce and adjust for seasoning.

16. Arrange the chicken over the bed of rainbow chard, then drizzle the sauce over the chicken.

17. For color and freshness, sprinkle the tomatoes all over the platter.

Variations

» *Use collard greens or kale instead of rainbow chard.*

» *Use thin boneless pork chops instead of chicken.*

GET YOUR GREENS!
(*THESE ARE MY FOUR FAVES.*)

Tuscan Kale
Dark blue-green and heavily textured, I tear it into soup, layer it in lasagna, or even grill the leaves for stunning veggie dishes (page 254).

Collard Greens
Collard leaves are tough and hearty, so I slow cook them with bacon or ham (page 279) or roll them up and slice the leaves thin to make a salad that stands up to any dressing.

Curly Kale
Previously relegated to salad bar garnish, curly kale is delightfully versatile as a star in salads, an add-in for scrambled eggs, or a pop of green in any pasta dish (page 249).

Swiss Chard
Bitter when raw, but mild after cooking, Swiss chard makes a beautiful bed of greens for any protein (page 161). A relative of the beet, the brightly colored stems have a flavor all their own!

CREAMY CHICKEN AND WILD RICE SOUP

MAKES 8 TO 10 SERVINGS

WHAT: A hearty chicken soup with wild rice, kale, and an herby cranberry sauce.

WHEN: A cool fall evening (or a frigid winter evening!).

WHY: Because it tastes like autumn in a bowl. With a little Thanksgiving thrown in.

This is an epic chicken soup recipe. Using the standard dictionary definitions, it is epic in that it is "particularly impressive or remarkable." It is also epic in that it is "heroic or grand in scale or character." But (keepin' it real here) it is also epic in that it is "a long work covering an extended period of time." This recipe takes a while to make! But yes, it is impressive, remarkable, heroic . . . and don't forget yummy!

1. Make the herby cranberry sauce: In a medium saucepan, combine all the ingredients for the sauce. Pour in 1 cup water . . .

3. Reduce the heat to low and cook, stirring occasionally, until most of the liquid has cooked down and the mixture is thick like jam. Set aside.

2. Then stir and bring to a gentle boil over medium heat.

4. Make the soup: Generously season the chicken with salt and pepper.

HERBY CRANBERRY SAUCE

12 ounces fresh or frozen cranberries

⅔ cup sugar

Juice of ½ lemon

½ teaspoon minced fresh thyme

½ teaspoon minced fresh rosemary

½ teaspoon minced fresh sage

Pinch of kosher salt

SOUP

3 pounds boneless, skinless chicken thighs

Kosher salt and black pepper

2 tablespoons olive oil

2 tablespoons butter

1 large yellow onion, halved and thinly sliced

3 large carrots, sliced into rounds

3 celery stalks, sliced

2 garlic cloves, minced

½ cup white wine (or low-sodium chicken broth)

⅓ cup all-purpose flour

4 cups (1 quart) low-sodium chicken broth

1 cup uncooked wild rice

1 bay leaf

1½ cups half-and-half

1 tablespoon minced fresh thyme

1 tablespoon minced fresh rosemary

1 tablespoon thinly sliced fresh sage leaves

1 bunch Tuscan (lacinato) kale, leaves torn into bite-size pieces

Juice of ½ lemon

5. Heat a large Dutch oven over medium-high heat and add the olive oil and butter. Working in two batches, brown the chicken on both sides . . .

6. Then remove it to a sheet pan or plate.

7. Add the onion, carrots, celery, and garlic to the pan. Stir and cook for 5 minutes, until the vegetables are slightly softened.

8. Add the wine and stir, scraping the bottom of the pan. Cook for 3 minutes, letting the wine reduce by at least half.

9. Reduce the heat to medium and sprinkle the flour over the vegetables . . .

10. Then stir for 2 minutes to let the flour start to cook.

11. Pour in the broth and 1 cup water . . .

12. And stir until the mixture is heated through, about 5 minutes.

13. Add the wild rice and stir it in . . .

14. Then add the chicken and any juices from the pan.

15. Finally, add the bay leaf.

16. Stir, reduce the heat to low, cover, and simmer until the wild rice is almost tender and the chicken is cooked through, about 35 minutes.

20. Then add the thyme, rosemary, sage . . .

23. Just before serving, remove the bay leaf, squeeze in the lemon juice, and stir! Taste and add more salt and/or pepper if needed.

17. Remove the chicken from the pot and shred it with two forks.

21. And kale.

24. Serve a big bowl of soup with a spoonful of the cranberry sauce on top.

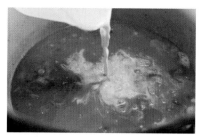

18. Pour the half-and-half into the soup and stir it to combine.

22. Stir the whole delicious mess together and let it simmer another 10 minutes. Taste the wild rice and make sure it's cooked completely. If not, add a little more water and let the soup simmer another 10 minutes.

Purely divine!

19. Return the chicken to the pot . . .

Halle, horseback.

Beef and Pork

Where's the beef? Well, it's right here, starring in a nice, big handful of scrumptious new vittles to feed your kinfolk. (I can't say "vittles" without also saying "kinfolk" in the same sentence.) You'll find a variety of cuts of beef in the pages to come, and different cooking methods as well. This is Ladd's favorite chapter! (Psst. I threw in a smaller handful of great pork recipes, too. Pork has a place at our table—just a slightly smaller place . . .)

LASAGNA SOUP

MAKES 8 TO 10 SERVINGS

WHAT: Beefy tomato soup with lasagna noodles and dollops of ricotta.

WHEN: When you have a hankering for both soup and lasagna . . . but you can't decide!

WHY: The soup is delicious, the noodles are big and bold, and the ricotta "dumplings" are such a yummy treat.

Lasagna is a go-to recipe in the ol' Drummond family, and there's nothing on earth that can top it. Unless, of course, you turn our go-to lasagna into a piping hot soup. It's a new favorite around here! Try it . . . just once. You'll see why.

12 uncooked lasagna noodles

3 tablespoons olive oil

1 yellow onion, halved and thinly sliced

4 garlic cloves, minced

1 tablespoon minced oregano

1 tablespoon minced thyme

1 pound ground beef

1 pound hot breakfast sausage

1 teaspoon kosher salt

½ teaspoon black pepper

3 tablespoons tomato paste

¾ cup white wine or stock

One 14.5-ounce can whole tomatoes with juice

4 cups (1 quart) vegetable or chicken stock

1 tablespoon chopped parsley, plus more for serving

½ cup heavy cream

RICOTTA "DUMPLINGS"

1 cup whole-milk ricotta cheese

½ cup freshly grated Parmesan cheese

1 tablespoon minced parsley

1 tablespoon minced basil

½ teaspoon kosher salt

½ teaspoon black pepper

1. Break the lasagna noodles into random smaller pieces.

3. In a large Dutch oven or soup pot, heat the olive oil over medium heat. Add the onion, garlic, oregano, and thyme and cook, stirring, until starting to soften, about 2 minutes.

2. Cook the noodles about 1 minute less than the package directions, until almost tender. Drain and set aside.

4. Increase the heat to medium-high, then add the ground beef, sausage, salt, and pepper . . .

5. And sauté until the meat is fully cooked, breaking it up as you go, about 5 minutes. Drain off at least half of the grease.

9. Add the tomatoes and their juice, crushing them with the spoon as you stir them in.

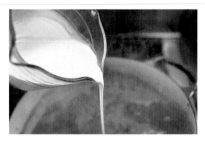

13. Pour in the cream and stir to combine.

6. Add the tomato paste . . .

10. Add the stock and stir it in . . .

14. Add the noodles and let them simmer for 5 minutes while you make the ricotta mixture.

7. And stir to combine. Let the tomato paste cook for 1 minute.

11. Then add the parsley.

15. Make the ricotta "dumplings": In a bowl, combine the ricotta, Parmesan, parsley, basil, salt, and pepper . . .

8. Add the wine and stir to deglaze the bottom of the pan, scraping up any flavorful little bits.

12. Bring to a boil, then reduce the heat to low and simmer for 20 minutes. Taste and adjust the salt and pepper as needed.

16. And stir until combined.

17. Dish up bowls of soup, sprinkle with a little extra parsley, and add a dollop of ricotta (or two or three) to the top of each one!

Variations

» *Use ground turkey.*
» *Omit the lasagna noodles for a lower-carb soup.*

Delicious and hearty!

Todd and my nephew Stu. Lasagna soup is right up their alley.

PORTOBELLO BUN BURGERS

MAKES 4 SMALL BURGERS

WHAT: Small-but-mighty burgers with mushrooms as the buns!

WHEN: Tasty lunch, delicious dinner, game night on TV, summer barbecue!

WHY: Because if you love burgers but need to step away from the carbs, these will be your saving grace! (Spoiler: You won't miss the bun at all.)

It cracks me up to imagine a Drummond barbecue, with all the cowboys in place, napkins tucked into their plaid, pearlized-snap shirts, where I serve up a big platter of burgers served on—wait for it—*mushrooms* instead of buns. In fact, that very scene would make an award-winning *SNL* skit. I play it over and over in my head when I need a good chuckle, and sometimes I'm tempted to play it out in real life and film it so that I can become a YouTube sensation. So what if I'm approximately thirty-three years too old to be a YouTube sensation?!? This skit would definitely make me the exception to the rule!

But I digress. These bunless burgers are dreamy. I'm hooked!

1½ pounds ground beef

3 dashes of Worcestershire sauce

½ teaspoon kosher salt, plus more for sprinkling

½ teaspoon black pepper, plus more for sprinkling

Olive oil, for grilling

8 portobello mushrooms, stemmed and cleaned

½ cup freshly grated Swiss cheese

4 tablespoons Dijon mustard

4 butter lettuce leaves

8 slices Roma tomato

½ cup crispy jalapeños (such as French's)

1. Heat a grill pan over medium heat.

2. In a large bowl, combine the ground chuck, Worcestershire, salt, and pepper and mix thoroughly. Form the mixture into 4 patties.

3. Brush the grill pan generously with olive oil. Place the mushrooms on the grill pan, top side down, and sprinkle them with salt and pepper. Grill for about 4 minutes . . .

4. Then flip and grill on the second side until they're tender but still have a little structure, about 4 minutes longer.

5. Remove to a sheet pan, lightly cover them with foil, and set aside.

6. Increase the heat under the pan to medium-high and grill the burgers on both sides, 3 to 4 minutes per side.

7. Two minutes before the burgers are done, top each with one-quarter of the Swiss cheese.

8. Reduce the heat to low and let the cheese melt.

9. Match the mushrooms into pairs according to like sizes (they are usually varied in size). Squirt about ½ tablespoon Dijon into each mushroom.

10. Place a burger on 4 of the mushrooms.

11. Add 1 lettuce leaf, 2 tomato slices, jalapeños, and top with the other 4 mushrooms.

Who needs buns? These are absolutely scrumptious!

Sticky, delicious, and fast!

INSTANT POT STICKY PORK LETTUCE WRAPS

MAKES 8 TO 10 SERVINGS

WHAT: The stickiest shredded pork in the universe, served in lettuce wraps.

WHEN: Dinner with friends (it's interactive and fun!).

WHY: The sweetness of the sticky pork and the cool, fresh lettuce are the perfect combo.

My original idea for this lettuce wrap recipe was to use a traditional barbecued pulled pork. But, as happens often when I start on a recipe, my scattered brain (and spice cabinet) took me in a totally different direction, and by the time I was finished, I'd made a sticky hoisin-based pork dish that is so beautifully unusual, it was hard to get it out of my mind for weeks. The flavor is incredible, and will make you fall in love with five-spice powder forever. Make this and set out all the elements when you have friends over. Building the wraps is part of the experience!

PICKLED ONIONS

½ cup rice vinegar (or any white vinegar)

1 teaspoon kosher salt

2 tablespoons sugar

Pinch of red pepper flakes

1 large red onion, halved and thinly sliced

PORK RUB

2 tablespoons packed brown sugar

2 teaspoons five-spice powder

2 teaspoons ground ginger

1 teaspoon garlic powder

1 teaspoon dry mustard

2 teaspoons kosher salt

1 teaspoon black pepper

PORK AND STICKY SAUCE

2 pounds boneless pork shoulder

1 tablespoon olive oil

1 tablespoon salted butter

1 cup low-sodium chicken stock

¼ cup hoisin sauce

¼ cup soy sauce

3 tablespoons rice vinegar

2 tablespoons Thai sweet chili sauce

1 tablespoon sriracha sauce, or more to taste

½ cup packed brown sugar

1 tablespoon cornstarch

FOR SERVING

Leaves from 2 to 3 heads Bibb or Boston lettuce

Toasted sesame seeds (see page 80)

3 green onions, sliced

1. First, make the pickled onions: In a small saucepan, combine the vinegar, salt, sugar, pepper flakes, and ½ cup water and bring to a boil over medium-low heat.

2. Place the onion in a large heatproof bowl and pour the mixture on top.

3. Cover and let it sit in the fridge until the pork is ready for serving. (Psst. You can make these a couple of days in advance!)

4. Make the pork rub: In a large bowl, place all the rub ingredients . . .

5. And whisk until combined.

6. Place the pork in the bowl, pressing the rub into the surface . . .

7. And keep going until the pork is completely coated in the rub.

8. Set the Instant Pot to Sauté. When it's hot, add the olive oil and butter, then place the pork in the pot.

9. Sear the pork on all sides until very brown, about 2 minutes per side. Remove it to a plate.

10. Add the stock to the Instant Pot and stir to scrape the browned bits from the bottom of the pot.

11. Add the hoisin, soy sauce, vinegar, sweet chili sauce, and sriracha . . .

12. And whisk until combined.

13. Return the pork to the pot.

14. Secure the lid on the pot and set the pressure valve to Sealing. Press the Manual button and set to 30 minutes.

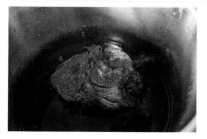

15. After the cook time, let the pressure release naturally for 10 minutes, then use the handle of a wooden spoon to open the valve to Venting, to let the rest of the pressure release quickly. Remove the lid . . .

16. And place the pork on a sheet pan.

17. Use two forks to shred the pork. Set it aside.

18. Set the Instant Pot back to Sauté, then add the brown sugar.

19. In a small bowl, whisk ½ cup water into the cornstarch.

20. Pour the mixture into the pot, then let it cook and bubble up for 2 to 3 minutes, stirring often.

21. It should be nice and thick. Taste and add more salt as needed.

22. Return the shredded pork to the sauce . . .

23. And stir until the pork is heated through and seriously sticky!

24. Serve the pork with the pickled onions, lettuce leaves, and sesame seeds. Sprinkle sliced green onions on top.

STANDARD COOKING DIRECTIONS

Preheat the oven to 300°F. Sear the pork in a Dutch oven, following steps 9 to 13. Add 1 cup extra stock or water and cover the pot. Braise for 3 to 3½ hours, until the pork is falling apart. Follow steps 16 to 24 to finish the pork and sauce.

Variation

» *Serve the pork over cooked white rice and top with sliced green onions.*

CREAMY LEMON PASTA WITH PANCETTA AND PEAS

MAKES 6 SERVINGS

WHAT: A heavenly pasta dish with a sprinkling of crisp golden crumbs.

WHEN: Pasta night! (Translation: Every night.)

WHY: The creamy lemon sauce with pancetta and peas is delicious enough, but the crispy golden crumb topping will become a new regular on top of all your quick pasta dishes!

This pasta dish is the kind of thing I crave when I need someone to hold me and tell me that everything's going to be okay and carbs are still allowed in this world. It's comforting, it's creamy, it's crazy-good, with a creamy lemon sauce and tons of flavor coming from little cubes of pancetta, an Italian bacon. But what will really knock your socks off is the crispy panko topping, sprinkled over the top of each serving as one would normally sprinkle on Parmesan. The crunchy texture is the perfect match for the creamy pasta, and I predict you're gonna fall in love! I sure did.

12 ounces orecchiette pasta

CRISPY CRUMBS

3 tablespoons salted butter

½ cup panko breadcrumbs

2 teaspoons grated lemon zest

Leaves from 1 thyme sprig

Pinch of kosher salt

Pinch of black pepper

PANCETTA AND PEAS

8 tablespoons (1 stick) salted butter

½ yellow onion, diced

2 garlic cloves, minced

1 cup cubed pancetta

1 teaspoon minced fresh thyme leaves

Grated zest and juice of 2 lemons

¾ cup heavy cream

2 cups frozen green peas, not thawed

1 cup grated Pecorino-Romano cheese

½ teaspoon kosher salt

½ teaspoon black pepper

1. Cook the pasta according to the package directions. Drain and set aside, reserving 2 cups of the hot cooking water.

3. And stir to coat the crumbs in the butter. Add the thyme, salt, and pepper . . .

2. Meanwhile, make the crispy crumbs: In a medium skillet, melt the butter over medium-low heat. Add the panko and lemon zest . . .

4. And continue to stir and toast the crumbs slowly, until they're deep golden brown, 4 to 5 minutes. Remove them from the pan and set them aside.

5. In a large deep skillet, melt the butter over medium-high heat. Add the onion, garlic, pancetta, and thyme leaves . . .

9. Pour in that gorgeous cream . . .

13. When the sauce is hot, add the Pecorino-Romano, salt, and pepper . . .

6. And cook, stirring often, until the pancetta is sizzling and the onion is soft, 5 to 6 minutes. Turn the heat to medium-low.

10. And stir. Gently simmer 2 to 3 minutes.

14. And the pasta . . .

7. Add the lemon zest and juice . . .

11. Add the peas . . .

15. And stir until combined and warmed. Taste and adjust the seasonings. If the sauce is too thick, splash in some reserved pasta water and stir.

Variation

» **Make a meatless pasta by simply omitting the pancetta!**

8. And stir to combine.

12. And stir to thaw and heat them, about 3 minutes.

16. Serve in individual pasta bowls with a generous sprinkling of crispy crumbs.

MY FAVORITE PASTA SHAPES

Rotini

My go-to noodle for mac and cheese or any cheese sauce. The thin curly shape holds on to the sauce, and it's always a fun shape for kids (and grown-ups!).

Farfalle

The most versatile noodle in my arsenal, bowtie-shaped pasta works well for elegant mushroom-and-wine sauces or everyday jars of marinara.

Thin Spaghetti

Thicker than angel hair but not as thick as regular spaghetti, this is the pasta I reach for when I need something twirly and light. Great for a tomato cream, primavera, or buttery clam sauce.

Radiatore

More off the beaten path, these noodles look like little radiators (hence the name) but are delightfully ruffled, making them just right for cold pasta salads.

PASTA ALLA LADD

MAKES 6 TO 8 SERVINGS

WHAT: My husband's favorite pasta dish! Rigatoni with rustic meat sauce.

WHEN: Weeknight dinner, or double or triple it to feed a crowd.

WHY: It's meaty, hearty, and wonderful.

Ladd has loved this pasta dish for over twenty years, because . . . well, the sauce is mostly made of meat. I started cooking it for him early in our marriage after basing it on a dish I remembered my mom making, and it's been true love ever since. Between Ladd and the pasta, I mean.

There are two things that set this apart from a traditional meat sauce: One, while it does boast big chunks of tomato throughout the sauce, the base is primarily meat and it isn't overwhelmingly saucy. Two, the sauce is highlighted not with the typical mix of Italian herbs but with wonderfully aromatic ground thyme. It sets it apart!

2 tablespoons olive oil	1 teaspoon red pepper flakes	1½ pounds rigatoni (or any chunky pasta)
1 medium onion, diced	½ teaspoon kosher salt, or more to taste	¼ cup freshly grated Parmesan cheese, for serving
3 garlic cloves, minced	½ teaspoon black pepper, or more to taste	Fresh basil leaves, for serving
2 pounds ground beef	Two 14-ounce cans whole tomatoes with juice	
1 teaspoon ground thyme		

1. In a large pot, heat the olive oil over medium-low heat. Add the onion and cook until starting to turn translucent, a couple of minutes. Add the garlic . . .

2. Along with the ground beef . . .

3. And cook until the meat is browned, crumbling as you go. Drain off most of the excess fat.

4. Add the thyme, pepper flakes, salt, black pepper, and tomatoes. Stir, breaking up the tomatoes with the spoon, then turn the heat to low, and cover the pot. Cook for 30 minutes, stirring occasionally . . .

5. Then uncover the pot and cook for 30 minutes more. Taste and adjust the salt and pepper if needed. Keep warm.

6. Cook the rigatoni according to the package directions and drain.

7. Place the pasta in individual bowls and spoon plenty of sauce over the top. Add grated Parmesan and fresh basil!

Skiing selfie!

INSTANT POT MEATLOAF

MAKES 6 SERVINGS

WHAT: Delicious, moist meatloaf made in less than an hour.

WHEN: When you have to have meatloaf in a jiff.

WHY: Because meatloaf made in less than an hour will change your life.

Meatloaf has my vote for one of the top ten comfort foods of all time. But it isn't something you can normally whip up on a moment's notice. Even if you can get the ingredients mushed together in just a few minutes (and it's realistic that you can), the chances are good that the meatloaf will take a good hour-and-a-half-plus before it's finally done in the middle.

Enter: The Instant Pot! Cooking meatloaf using the pressure cooker feature is an absolute miracle. It remains moist and tender, and is always perfectly cooked in the middle. And while it doesn't have that signature top crust you might be used to, the beautiful, succulent texture more than makes up for it. This is the answer to all your meatloaf-craving fantasies.

MEATLOAF

6 slices bread

1 cup whole milk

2 pounds lean ground beef (90/10)

4 large eggs, beaten

1 cup grated Parmesan cheese

1 teaspoon kosher salt

1 teaspoon black pepper

¼ teaspoon seasoned salt, such as Lawry's

⅓ cup minced parsley, plus more for serving

TOMATO SAUCE

½ cup ketchup

6 tablespoons packed brown sugar

1 teaspoon dry mustard

A couple dashes of Worcestershire sauce

A few dashes of hot sauce

1. For the meatloaf: Place the bread in a large bowl and pour the milk on top. Let the bread absorb the milk for a few minutes.

3. And mix with clean hands or a wooden spoon until thoroughly combined. Set aside.

2. Add the ground beef, eggs, Parmesan, salt, pepper, seasoned salt, and parsley . . .

4. For the tomato sauce: In a separate bowl, combine the ketchup, brown sugar, dry mustard, Worcestershire, and hot sauce. Stir until smooth.

5. Form the meat mixture into a loaf shape about 5 x 7 inches. Place the loaf in the center of a 24-inch piece of heavy-duty foil. Fold up the sides to create a form that will help support the meatloaf, folding the long ends so that they can be used as "handles" to lift out the meatloaf after it's cooked. Place the trivet inside the Instant Pot (it comes with the machine!) and set the foil and meatloaf contraption on top of the trivet.

6. Spoon half of the tomato sauce over the meatloaf, reserving the rest.

7. Carefully pour 1 cup water into the bottom of the Instant Pot, being careful not to pour it on the meatloaf. Secure the lid and set the pressure valve to Sealing. Press the Manual button and set to 40 minutes.

8. When the cook time is up, use the handle of a wooden spoon to move the valve to Venting to let the pressure release quickly. Remove the lid.

9. Remove the meatloaf from the Instant Pot and peel back the foil. Slice the meatloaf and brush on one-quarter of the remaining sauce.

10. Serve with a sprinkle of parsley and the remaining sauce on the side.

STANDARD COOKING INSTRUCTIONS

Form the meat mixture into a loaf shape, add half the sauce to the top, and place on a broiler pan (or a pan with a rack). Bake in a preheated 350°F oven for 45 minutes. Add the rest of the sauce to the top and bake until the meatloaf is cooked through to the center, an additional 20 minutes. Slice and serve.

Say cheese, Tim!
(Guess he didn't hear me . . .)

BUNLESS CHILI CHEESEBURGER

MAKES 6 SERVINGS

WHAT: A drippy, sinful chili cheeseburger . . . without the sin of bread!

WHEN: When you want to dive into something crazy indulgent, but without the carbs.

WHY: Because this is the one chili cheeseburger on the face of the earth you don't have to feel guilty about.

There's a restaurant in Vail, Colorado, that my family and I have visited for years. It's called Bart & Yeti's, and what we love about it is that it's seriously casual and unpretentious as ski resort restaurants go—a place we could feel comfortable taking the kids when they were energetic little boogers and a place the kids still love now that they're all six hundred feet tall. Bart & Yeti's has lots of good, American bar food, but the most delicious menu item, hands down, is their chili cheeseburger. It's a triumph. So this is an ode to Bart, to Yeti, to Vail, Colorado . . . and to leaving off the bun, which you'll never notice because there is a ton of cheese on top. Here's to making healthy choices!

5 pounds ground beef

Kosher salt and black pepper

½ medium yellow onion, roughly chopped

3 garlic cloves, minced

One 14.5-ounce can diced tomatoes with juice

One 6-ounce can tomato paste

2 tablespoons chili powder

2 teaspoons ground cumin

8 ounces sharp Cheddar cheese, grated

½ cup sour cream, for serving

½ medium red onion, roughly chopped, for serving

1. Preheat the oven to 175°F.

2. Form 2½ pounds of the ground beef into 6 equal-size patties, each about ½ inch thick. Season both sides with salt and pepper.

5. Crumble and cook the beef until it's completely done, then drain off the excess grease.

8. Remove the burger patties from the oven and place each one on a plate. Top each with Cheddar, chili, sour cream, and red onion.

3. Working in two batches, fry the patties in a large skillet over medium heat. Cook until the burgers are done in the middle, about 3 minutes per side. Remove the patties to a sheet pan, cover lightly with foil, and put in the oven to keep warm.

6. Add the diced tomatoes and their juice, tomato paste, chili powder, and cumin. Fill the diced tomato can with water and pour it in.

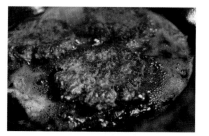

4. To the same skillet, add the remaining 2½ pounds ground beef, the onion, garlic, ½ teaspoon salt, and ½ teaspoon pepper. Increase the heat to medium-high.

7. Stir and cook until bubbling, about 20 minutes. Taste and adjust the seasoning.

(Psst. For heartier appetites, make three doubles instead!)

Variation

» *Substitute ground turkey for the ground beef.*

CAST-IRON PIZZA

MAKES ONE 12-INCH PIZZA

WHAT: A crispy-edged pizza baked in an insanely hot skillet.

WHEN: Any time you have a ball of pizza dough on hand!

WHY: Because nothing makes that crust sizzle quite like a 500°F chunk of iron.

In our pizza joint in our town of Pawhuska, we have a pizza oven whose temperature can get as high as 1,300°F. A raging fire burns inside, and once when I was trying to be cute, I reached my iPhone into the opening to take a slo-mo video of the crackling flames. The hair on my hands still hasn't grown back.

Anyway, we bake our pizzas at around 750°F at the restaurant, which makes for the most pleasantly perfect edge of crust. And while it's hard to achieve that same effect in a conventional home oven, I've found that this cast-iron method comes as close as you can get. It's all about the sizzle!

½ recipe pizza dough
(see Not Knots, page 99), or
use store-bought pizza dough

¼ cup olive oil, plus more
for brushing

½ cup store-bought pizza or
marinara sauce

6 ounces fresh mozzarella pearls

¾ cup sliced pepperoni

¼ cup torn basil leaves

1. Position racks in the center and lower third of the oven and preheat it to 500°F. Place a 12-inch cast-iron skillet on the center rack. Let it heat for 10 minutes.

3. Roll or stretch the dough into a 14-inch round.

5. Then carefully transfer the dough to the skillet, pressing it up the edges using a wooden spoon. Don't worry if the dough shrinks back a bit.

2. Form the dough into a tight ball and place it on the counter.

4. Using very thick hot pads, carefully remove the skillet from the oven and place it on a towel on a heatproof surface. Drizzle two-thirds of the olive oil into the skillet . . .

6. Spread the sauce over the dough, leaving a ½-inch border uncovered.

7. Cover the sauce with mozzarella pearls . . .

9. Brush the exposed dough edge with the remaining olive oil, then bake on the bottom rack of the oven until golden brown, 12 to 13 minutes.

Transfer to a cutting board, top with torn basil, cut into slices, and serve.

8. Then cover the pearls with the pepperoni! I used large and small, just for fun.

MY FAVORITE PIZZA TOPPINGS

Add these to elevate a regular pepperoni pizza, or mix them up to create your own perfect combination!

✿ *Caramelized Onions*
Cook sliced yellow onions in butter over medium-low heat until dark and delicious.

✿ *Sautéed Mushrooms*
Cook quartered white button mushrooms in butter, garlic, and red wine over medium heat until the mushrooms are cooked and the liquid is mostly evaporated.

✿ *Roasted Eggplant*
Cut a small eggplant into 1-inch dice. Sprinkle with salt and let rest on paper towels for 30 minutes to drain. Drizzle the eggplant with olive oil and roast on a sheet pan at 425°F for 20 minutes.

✿ *Halved Cherry Tomatoes*
Toss them with a little olive oil, balsamic, salt, pepper, and basil leaves cut into a chiffonade. Scatter the tomatoes over the pizza after it comes out of the oven!

✿ *Goat Cheese*
Add crumbles of goat cheese to the top after the pizza comes out of the oven. Delicious.

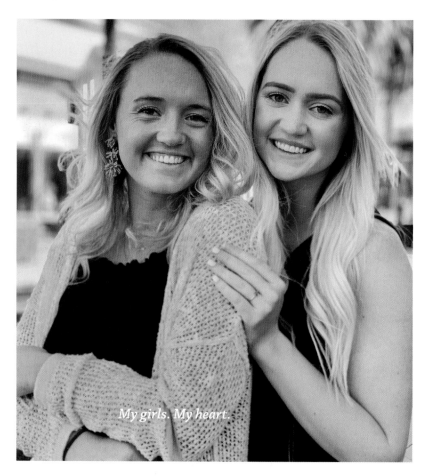

My girls. My heart.

RANCH PORK CHOP SHEET PAN SUPPER

MAKES 4 SERVINGS

WHAT: Flavorful glazed pork chops baked alongside potatoes and green beans.

WHEN: When you can't be bothered to stand at the stove! (And when you need a tasty, family-friendly meal.)

WHY: Because it's a cinch to throw in the oven, and it looks really neat and tidy on the sheet pan, for those of you who rejoice at things like that.

This is a winner of a sheet pan dinner, and so easy to pull together. It's a no-frills meal that's just the thing for a quiet weeknight. Or a crazy weeknight. Or a silly weeknight. Whichever applies!

2 tablespoons honey

2 tablespoons Worcestershire sauce

One 3.5-ounce packet ranch dressing mix

5 tablespoons olive oil

1½ teaspoons kosher salt

1½ teaspoons black pepper

4 boneless pork chops (about 6 ounces each)

1½ pounds baby Yukon Gold potatoes, halved lengthwise

8 ounces green beans, trimmed

Chopped parsley, for serving

1. Preheat the oven to 475°F.

2. In a small bowl, whisk the honey, Worcestershire, 2 tablespoons of the ranch dressing mix, 2 tablespoons of the olive oil, ½ teaspoon of the salt, and 1 teaspoon of the pepper.

3. Place the pork chops on one end of a sheet pan and brush the mixture on both sides.

4. In a medium bowl, combine the potatoes, 2 tablespoons of the remaining olive oil, 1 tablespoon of the ranch dressing mix, ½ teaspoon of the remaining salt, and ¼ teaspoon of the remaining pepper. Toss to coat.

5. Place the potatoes in the center of the sheet pan next to the pork chops. Roast the chops and potatoes for 15 minutes.

8. Return the pan to the oven and roast until the pork chops are done and the veggies are browned, 7 to 8 minutes. Garnish with the parsley and serve.

6. Meanwhile, add the beans to the same bowl and add the remaining 1 tablespoon olive oil, remaining ranch mix, remaining ½ teaspoon salt, and remaining ¼ teaspoon pepper. Toss to coat and set aside.

Variations

» *Substitute chicken cutlets for the pork chops.*
» *Substitute cubed butternut squash or a mix of root vegetables for the potatoes.*
» *Substitute broccoli florets for the green beans.*

7. When the 15 minutes are up, remove the sheet pan from the oven. Using metal tongs, flip the pork chops and brush them generously with more glaze. Use the tongs to turn the potatoes, then spread the green beans in the empty space on the sheet pan.

He just can't control his tongue.

Short ribs in a jiffy!

INSTANT POT SHORT RIB POT ROAST

MAKES 4 TO 6 SERVINGS

WHAT: Fall-off-the-bone short ribs cooked in wine and stock . . . in around an hour!

WHEN: A casual or elegant dinner. It straddles the line between both!

WHY: Because short ribs done in an hour are a game changer.

To channel Sandy in *Grease*, and please imagine that I have a sweet singing voice, which I don't: "I'm hopelessly devoted to short ribs." They are my favorite cut of beef, and I highly encourage you to work them into your pot roast rotation whenever you're able to swap them in for your regular pot roast cut. They're mind-blowing and crazy-good, and cooking them in a pressure cooker means they wind up on your plate a lot faster. Amen!

8 bone-in short ribs (about 3 pounds total)

Kosher salt and black pepper

2 tablespoons olive oil

2 tablespoons salted butter

2 onions, quartered

3 carrots, cut into 1½-inch chunks

3 celery stalks, cut into 1½-inch chunks

6 garlic cloves, peeled

1 cup red wine (or more beef stock)

1 cup beef stock

4 thyme sprigs

2 rosemary sprigs

Mashed potatoes (page 269), for serving

Wilted Spinach (recipe follows), for serving

1. Set the Instant Pot to Sauté on high.

2. Season the short ribs generously with salt and pepper.

3. When the Instant Pot is hot, add the oil and butter. Working in batches, sear the short ribs on all sides. Remove them to a plate.

4. Add the onions, carrots, celery, and garlic and cook, stirring often, until the veggies start to soften, about 5 minutes.

5. Pour in the wine and use a wooden spoon to scrape up any bits on the bottom of the pan.

7. Then return the short ribs to the pot. Secure the lid and set the pressure valve to Sealing. Press the Manual button and set to 45 minutes.

9. The short ribs should almost be falling off the bone.

6. Add the stock and herbs . . .

8. When the cook time is up, let the pressure release naturally for 15 minutes, then use the handle of a wooden spoon to move the valve to Venting, to let the rest of the pressure release. Remove the lid.

10. Serve 2 short ribs and a few veggies over mashed potatoes and wilted spinach (see below). Spoon the cooking liquid over the top.

STANDARD COOKING INSTRUCTIONS

Follow the instructions for searing the short ribs, except use a Dutch oven over medium-high heat. Add the rest of the ingredients, increasing the stock to 2 cups, then reduce the heat to low. Cover the Dutch oven and simmer the short ribs until tender, about 2 hours 30 minutes. Serve as directed.

WILTED SPINACH

In a large skillet, heat 1 tablespoon olive oil over medium heat. Add 5 ounces baby spinach (in batches if needed) and cook until wilted, about 2 minutes, using tongs to move the wilted spinach on top. The spinach is done when it's wilted but hasn't given up entirely. Sprinkle with salt and pepper and serve.

STEAKHOUSE PASTA

MAKES 6 SERVINGS

WHAT: Grilled steak served alongside pappardelle pasta in a creamy tomato-brandy sauce.

WHEN: Pasta night, or any other monumentally special occasion.

WHY: The sauce is so indescribably scrumptious, you'll forget what your middle name is.

My knees go weak whenever I'm in the presence of a creamy pasta sauce. And I'm particularly susceptible to the powers of a creamy *tomato* sauce (some call it "pink sauce" because of the combo of white and red). But take that creamy tomato sauce and spike it with a little brandy? Yeah, you guessed it: I'm a goner. I'm toast. I cease to exist. I'm a pool of nothingness on the floor. And don't get me started on what happens if you add sliced grilled steak to this scenario. Not kidding, I actually disintegrate into thin air. Like in the movie *Night of the Comet*, only it's caused by food instead of a deadly meteor.

Enjoy this recipe! I sure would if I still existed.

- 1½ pounds pappardelle pasta
- 2 tablespoons olive oil
- 3 garlic cloves, minced
- ½ cup brandy
- One 28-ounce can diced tomatoes, drained
- ½ teaspoon sugar
- Kosher salt
- ¾ teaspoon black pepper, or more to taste

- ¼ teaspoon red pepper flakes, or to taste
- Vegetable oil, for the grill pan
- ½ teaspoon seasoned salt, such as Lawry's
- ½ teaspoon lemon-pepper seasoning
- ¾ pound skirt steak
- ¾ cup heavy cream

- 1 tablespoon prepared horseradish
- 1 tablespoon crumbled blue cheese
- ¾ cup freshly grated Fontina cheese
- 3 cups packed baby spinach
- 12 basil leaves, for serving

1. Cook the pappardelle according to the package directions. Drain and set aside.

2. Meanwhile, in a large, deep skillet, heat the olive oil over medium heat. Add the garlic and cook for a minute, stirring so it won't burn.

3. Remove from the heat and pour in the brandy. Return to medium heat and simmer until the brandy is reduced by half, stirring occasionally, about 4 minutes.

4. Add the tomatoes . . .

5. And stir to combine. Add the sugar, ¼ teaspoon kosher salt, ¼ teaspoon of the pepper, and the pepper flakes. Cook for 10 minutes, stirring occasionally.

6. Brush a grill pan with the vegetable oil and heat to medium-high.

7. While the pan heats up, in a small bowl, combine the seasoned salt, lemon-pepper seasoning, remaining ½ teaspoon pepper, and a pinch of kosher salt.

8. Sprinkle half the seasonings on one side of the steak and place it seasoned side down on the hot grill pan. Sprinkle the other side with the rest of the seasonings.

9. Cook the steak for 3 minutes, then flip it to the other side and cook for 2 minutes, until medium-rare. Set the steak on a board to rest.

13. And the Fontina . . .

17. And toss everything together. (The spinach will start to wilt immediately!) Cook the pasta on low for a minute to make sure everything is perfect.

10. Back to the sauce! Reduce the heat to low, pour in the cream . . .

14. And stir until the cheeses are totally melted into the sauce.

18. Cut the steak into strips against the grain . . .

11. And stir to combine, then let the sauce heat back up.

15. Add the spinach . . .

12. Add the horseradish, the blue cheese . . .

16. And the pasta . . .

19. And serve it up alongside the pasta, with fresh basil on top.

Daylilies remind me of Ladd's mom, Nan. She loved them.

Seafood

More and more, surf is making an appearance on Drummond turf. Of all the varieties, shrimp is still the seafood choice I reach for the most, but cod, tilapia, and salmon are definitely vying for my attention! This chapter will show you some easy and tasty choices for upping your family's seafood game. I won't tell you which recipe is my favorite . . . because there's no way I'd be able to choose!

QUICK SHRIMP AND GRITS

MAKES 6 SERVINGS

WHAT: Creamy, cheesy grits with saucy shrimp on top.

WHEN: Weeknight dinner, weekend brunch, or appetizer (if served in tiny bowls).

WHY: Because the combination of the spicy shrimp and creamy grits is a love language all its own.

Out of respect for tradition, I would never claim this dish as the gold standard for the classic Southern dish, but I will say that it's good enough for me. And by "good enough," I mean that it's absolutely one of my top ten favorite dishes of all time. It's one of those recipes that tempts me and taunts me as I'm cooking it, the kind of recipe that sometimes doesn't even make it into the bowl because I can't keep myself from diving in. It also happens to be a looker of a dinner, perfect when you want to treat yourself to something special, but also casually elegant for guests. (Have I mentioned I love this recipe?)

5 cups low-sodium chicken broth

¾ cup quick-cooking grits

½ cup mascarpone or cream cheese

1½ cups grated pepper Jack cheese

1½ cups grated sharp Cheddar cheese

4 tablespoons (½ stick) salted butter

1½ pounds jumbo shrimp, peeled, deveined, and tails removed

1 tablespoon Cajun seasoning

1 tablespoon olive oil

6 slices bacon, chopped

1 medium yellow onion, diced

1 red bell pepper, seeded and diced

1 jalapeño, partially seeded and minced

Kosher salt and black pepper

2 tablespoons tomato paste

Hot sauce

Juice of ½ lemon

2 green onions, sliced, for serving

1. In a saucepan, bring 3 cups of the chicken broth to a boil over medium-high heat. Slowly whisk in the grits. (Heat the remaining 2 cups broth in a separate saucepan over medium-low heat. Keep warm.)

2. Cook for 3 minutes, whisking regularly.

3. Reduce the heat to low and add the mascarpone, pepper Jack, and Cheddar. Cook, stirring often, for 3 minutes, until the grits are tender.

4. Stir in 2 tablespoons of the butter, set aside, and cover the pot to keep the grits warm.

5. Season the shrimp with the Cajun seasoning.

6. In a large skillet, heat the oil and the remaining 2 tablespoons butter over medium-high heat. Add the shrimp to the skillet . . .

7. And cook for 1 to 2 minutes on each side, until the shrimp are golden and not quite done. Remove the shrimp from the skillet and set aside on a plate.

8. Add the bacon, onion, bell pepper, and jalapeño to the skillet and season with salt and black pepper. Cook, stirring often, until the bacon is cooked but not crisp and the veggies are browned, about 3 minutes. Drain the excess grease.

9. Add the tomato paste, stir it in, and cook for another minute.

10. Pour in the reserved hot broth and add hot sauce to taste. Bring the liquid to a boil . . .

11. Then return the shrimp to the skillet with any juices that collected on the plate. Let simmer until the shrimp are done, another 2 minutes.

12. Squeeze on the lemon juice, then taste and adjust the seasoning as desired.

13. To serve, scoop the grits into bowls and spoon the shrimp and sauce on top. Sprinkle with the green onions.

Variations

» **Omit the grits for a lower-carb option and serve the shrimp with cooked spinach or greens.**

» **Serve the shrimp open-faced on a toasted bun for a twist on a po'boy!**

FISH ALMONDINE

MAKES 6 SERVINGS

WHAT: Light, flaky cod with a crispy almond crumb topping.

WHEN: Weeknight family dinner, weekend dinner for guests.

WHY: Because fish is good for ya! (And the topping is totes tasty.)

From when I was expecting my first baby, Alex, to well past the birth of my second child, Paige, I used to meet my grandmother, Ga-Ga, at Luby's Cafeteria in my hometown for lunch on an almost monthly basis. Luby's had a mega-long (it seemed like a football field, but probably wasn't quite) serving line of prefilled small plates holding such comfort foods as Jell-O salad, macaroni and cheese, Salisbury steak, fried chicken, mashed potatoes, and slices of pie as far as the eye could see. But for me, the single most memorable dish at Luby's was their gloriously consistent Fish Almondine. No matter which seventeen sides I selected (okay, sometimes it was eighteen), Fish Almondine was always the main course for me. This is my best attempt to re-create the Luby's magic. (I love and miss you, Ga-Ga.)

¾ cup panko breadcrumbs

⅓ cup sliced almonds

3 tablespoons salted butter, melted

2 tablespoons chopped parsley

Kosher salt and black pepper

⅓ cup all-purpose flour

Six 6-ounce cod fillets

½ cup mayonnaise

Juice of 1 lemon

1. Preheat the oven to 375°F.

2. In a small bowl, combine the panko and almonds. Drizzle in the melted butter and toss until well combined.

3. Add the parsley and toss it in . . .

4. Then stir in ½ teaspoon salt and ¼ teaspoon pepper.

Instant Pot
Mashed Potatoes
(page 269)

Light, crispy, buttery, wonderful!

5. Put the flour in a shallow dish and add a pinch each of salt and pepper. Stir to combine.

7. Spread a generous tablespoon of mayonnaise over each piece of fish . . .

9. Bake until the crumbs are golden and the fish is flaky, 16 to 18 minutes. Squeeze the lemon juice on top and serve.

6. Dredge both sides of the fish in the flour, shaking off any excess.

8. And sprinkle the crumb mixture on top, pressing lightly to make sure it sticks.

Variation

» *Add ¼ cup grated Parmesan cheese to the crumb mixture.*

HOST A "CAFETERIA" DINNER PARTY!

I celebrate cafeterias. They remind me of meals with my grandmother, and of a simpler time, when food was about being tasty, homey, and decidedly non-gourmet. Here is my list of can't-miss cafeteria essentials. Pick and choose to make your own cafeteria-style dinner menu.

Jell-O: Any color goes! Best if cut into cubes and served in small bowls.

Fried Okra: Little coins of okra, breaded in seasoned cornmeal, fried to a deep golden, and lightly salted.

Macaroni and Cheese: Large elbow macaroni is preferred, as is a cheese blend that contains velvety-smooth, processed cheese.

Spinach: Boiled or sautéed, with bits of ham and onion and plenty of seasoning.

Chopped Steak: Ground beef or "chopped" seasoned steak, fried until medium-well and topped with an abundance of savory brown gravy and onions. Yes, please!

Mashed Potatoes with Cream Gravy: Again, best served in small bowls, with a well in the center of the potatoes to make room for as much gravy as possible.

Sweet Cornbread: Baked in a 9 x 13-inch pan and cut into thick squares. A little honey butter on the side is required.

Slice of Any Pie: Chocolate cream, lemon meringue, Dutch apple, pecan, custard, butterscotch. Any pie your great-grandmother took to her church social is fair game.

SHEET PAN SHRIMP PUTTANESCA

MAKES 4 TO 6 SERVINGS

WHAT: An easy, breezy sheet pan dinner with shrimp, olives, tomatoes, and chunks of bread.

WHEN: When you're in the mood for a quick, flavorful shrimp dish!

WHY: Because roasting shrimp with bread cubes will be the best thing that'll happen to you all week.

Sheet pan suppers are a home cook's dream come true. The idea of throwing things onto a rimmed baking sheet, cooking it all together in the oven, then serving it off the same pan, is the very embodiment of easy cooking. This incredibly simple dinner is a nod to pasta puttanesca, but instead of pasta, it's baked with big, toasted bread cubes. During the course of the roasting process, this bread soaks up all the flavors of the shrimp, veggies, and salty olives, and you'll be hard pressed not to eat all the bread before you even start on the shrimp! I saw "a friend" do it once. And she didn't regret it at all.

1 red onion, cut into thin wedges

3 cups 1-inch cubes sourdough bread

1 pint cherry tomatoes

½ cup pitted Niçoise olives

4 tablespoons olive oil

Kosher salt and black pepper

1½ pounds jumbo shrimp, peeled, deveined, and tails removed

2 tablespoons red wine vinegar

1 anchovy, minced (optional)

1 tablespoon capers, drained

¼ cup parsley leaves

1. Preheat the oven to 375°F.

2. Arrange the onion, bread cubes, tomatoes, and olives on a sheet pan. Drizzle 2 tablespoons of the olive oil on top, season with salt and pepper, and toss everything together.

3. Bake until the bread starts to brown and crisp, 12 to 14 minutes.

4. In the meantime, in a medium bowl, toss the shrimp with 1 tablespoon of the olive oil and ½ teaspoon salt.

5. Arrange the shrimp over the bread-veggie mixture and bake until the shrimp is opaque, 8 to 9 minutes longer.

7. Stir in the capers.

9. Sprinkle on the parsley leaves and serve right off the sheet pan!

6. In a small bowl, whisk together the remaining 1 tablespoon olive oil, the vinegar, and the anchovy (if using).

8. Drizzle the dressing over the puttanesca and toss everything to coat.

Variations

» *Add Parmesan shavings over the top before serving.*

» *Use a mix of scallops, shrimp, and lobster for a special occasion.*

SHEET PAN ADDICT

Sheet pans are marvelous things. I can think of no other single item on which you bake cookies, roast chicken, bake cakes, cook bacon, make quiche, flash freeze, cook pizza, bake pie, and (have you ever done this?) cover a pot if you're missing a lid. I could not be a home cook without them.

One day, out of curiosity, I pulled out all my sheet pans so I could count how many I'd accumulated. The final count: twenty-eight! A little more than one per year since Ladd and I were married.

I don't trust a shiny new sheet pan. It needs to develop a worn patina (and a few hard water marks are okay, too). Dents tell a good story. Did I use this one to cover my head in a hailstorm?

And then there's this beauty, which was surely once on the outdoor grill, but now is used for roasted meats. A work of art.

I highly recommend starting a collection.

PARMESAN FISH STICKS

MAKES 12 TO 14 FISH STICKS (TO SERVE ABOUT 4)

WHAT: Crisp, flavorful oven-baked fish sticks.

WHEN: Weeknight dinner or "anytime" snack!

WHY: Because fish sticks will forever remind me (and anyone else born between 1950 and 1985) of my childhood.

My mom was a pretty darn good from-scratch home cook, but she wasn't afraid to whip out the fish sticks if she was in need of a quick weeknight meal. And by fish sticks I mean store-bought, *frozen* fish sticks. Growing up in a landlocked state, I'm fairly certain they were my first introduction to seafood. Anyway, here is my recipe for fish sticks you can make yourself, baked in the oven to a crispy, golden goodness. I'll be danged if they don't taste exactly like the 1974 originals!

2 tablespoons olive oil

2 pounds haddock or cod

1 cup all-purpose flour

1 teaspoon kosher salt

½ teaspoon black pepper

2 cups plain breadcrumbs

¼ cup chopped parsley

4 tablespoons (½ stick) salted butter, melted

½ cup grated Parmesan cheese (the fine powdery kind!)

3 large eggs

Ketchup, for serving

1. Preheat the oven to 450°F. Grease a sheet pan with the olive oil.

2. Cut the fish into strips about 2½ inches long and 1 inch thick.

3. In a shallow bowl, combine the flour, salt, and pepper. Stir and set aside.

4. In a separate bowl, combine the breadcrumbs, parsley, and melted butter. Stir with the fork until combined.

5. Add the Parmesan and stir to combine. Whisk the eggs in a third bowl.

8. And finally rolling it in the crumb mixture.

11. Bake for 10 minutes, then remove the pan and carefully turn the fish sticks over.

6. Bread the fish by dredging a piece in the flour mixture . . .

9. Repeat with the rest of the fish.

7. Then dunking it in the whisked eggs . . .

10. Arrange the fish sticks on the prepared pan.

12. Continue baking until the breading is deep golden and the fish is cooked through, 7 to 8 minutes longer.

Once a cowgirl, always a cowgirl.

13. Serve with ketchup! Yum yum.

SHRIMP SCAMPI LASAGNA ROLL-UPS

MAKES 8 TO 12 SERVINGS

WHAT: A delectable shrimp-and-pasta casserole with a rich, creamy sauce.

WHEN: When you're serving shrimp lovers. And pasta lovers. And cheese lovers!

WHY: You can make it all the way through if you have the time, or you can refrigerate or freeze the unbaked casserole for less fuss at dinnertime!

This casserole pretty much contains everything I stand for: Garlicky shrimp and ricotta filling. Creamy white sauce. Noodles. Mozzarella. The result, while it may take a few steps to get there, is a ridiculous explosion of comfort food fabulousness that you and your family (or friends . . . or whoever is lucky enough to be invited to your house for dinner that night) won't soon forget. Because of its richness, this isn't necessarily something you'll make every week, but we all need those special dishes we can break out when the occasion dictates!

LASAGNA

12 lasagna noodles

1½ cups grated fresh mozzarella cheese

FILLING

2 tablespoons salted butter

2 tablespoons olive oil

½ medium yellow onion, finely diced

3 garlic cloves, minced

1 teaspoon red pepper flakes

1 pound medium shrimp, peeled, deveined, and tails removed

Juice of 1 lemon

½ cup white wine (or you can use shrimp or veggie broth)

Kosher salt and black pepper

One 8-ounce package cream cheese, at room temperature

1 cup whole-milk ricotta cheese

½ cup freshly grated Parmesan cheese

1 large egg

2 tablespoons minced parsley, plus more for serving

SAUCE

4 tablespoons (½ stick) salted butter

2 tablespoons all-purpose flour

2 garlic cloves, minced

2 cups whole milk

1 cup heavy cream

¼ teaspoon kosher salt

¼ teaspoon black pepper

1. Prepare the lasagna: Cook the lasagna noodles just under al dente. Drain them and rinse them in cold water to stop the cooking process.

3. Meanwhile, prepare the filling: In a large skillet, heat the butter and olive oil over medium heat. Add the onion, garlic, and pepper flakes . . .

2. Lay the noodles out flat on a piece of foil or parchment so they will keep their shape.

4. And cook, stirring, until the onion is turning translucent, 2 to 3 minutes.

5. Add the shrimp . . .

6. And cook, stirring constantly, until turning pink, 1 to 2 minutes.

7. Add the lemon juice, wine, ½ teaspoon salt, and ½ teaspoon pepper . . .

8. And stir to combine. Let simmer until the shrimp are cooked through and the wine is almost fully reduced, about 1½ minutes. Remove from the heat and let cool slightly.

9. Chop the shrimp into bite-size pieces and set aside to cool. (Hold on to the skillet for making the sauce.)

10. In a large bowl, combine the cream cheese, ricotta, Parmesan, and egg.

11. Add the parsley and a pinch each of salt and pepper . . .

12. Then mix it all together with a rubber spatula . . .

13. And fold in the shrimp. Keep the filling in the fridge while you make the sauce.

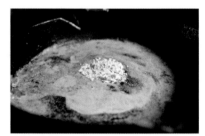

14. Make the sauce: In the same skillet you used to cook the shrimp, melt the butter. Add the flour and garlic . . .

15. And whisk and cook until the roux turns golden brown, about 3 minutes.

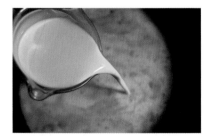

16. Pour in the milk, cream, salt, and pepper . . .

17. And whisk constantly until it's thick, about 3 minutes. Remove from the heat and let cool to lukewarm.

21. And place the roll seam side down in the pan.

24. To bake, preheat the oven to 375°F. Bake until golden and bubbling, about 25 minutes. Sprinkle on the parsley.

18. To assemble the lasagna, spread 1 cup of the sauce in the bottom of a 9 x 13-inch baking dish.

22. Repeat with the rest of the noodles, then pour the rest of the sauce over the top.

19. Working one at a time, spread about ½ cup of the shrimp filling over a lasagna noodle . . .

23. Top with the grated mozzarella. You can bake it immediately, or you can cover it and refrigerate it for up to 2 days before baking, or freeze it for up to 3 months (thaw it thoroughly in the fridge before baking).

25. Serve the roll-ups with a side of veggies. Divine!

20. Roll it up so that the filling is inside the noodle . . .

HERB CITRUS SALMON

MAKES 4 SERVINGS

WHAT: Fresh, citrusy parcels with tender salmon and bright, fresh veggies.

WHEN: A light summer meal or elegant dinner party.

WHY: Because a whole layer of citrus makes everything a little more lovely!

I didn't like salmon until my forties, and since I finally saw the light, I have been making up for lost time. The conclusion I've come to during this journey is that salmon is delicious, whether you roast it, sauté it, poach it, or grill it—and no matter what mix of flavors you adorn it with. These neat little foil parcels are positively citralicious, and also great to make for a dinner party, as you can assemble as many as you need and bake them all at once. I love you, salmon! I'm sorry I stayed away all those years. I had issues!

½ cup olive oil

4 tablespoons minced parsley

Leaves from 3 thyme sprigs, minced

1 tablespoon minced oregano leaves

Kosher salt and black pepper

1 bunch asparagus, tough ends removed, cut into 1-inch segments

2 carrots, sliced on a diagonal

1 cup cherry tomatoes, halved

Four 6-ounce skinless salmon fillets

1 lemon, halved lengthwise and thinly sliced

1 lime, halved lengthwise and thinly sliced

1 orange, halved lengthwise and thinly sliced

1. Preheat the oven to 450°F. Cut four 12 x 12-inch pieces of foil.

2. In a small bowl, whisk together the olive oil, 2 tablespoons of the parsley, the thyme, oregano, and a dash of salt and pepper.

3. Place the asparagus, carrots, and cherry tomatoes in a medium bowl. Add half the herb mixture . . .

4. And toss to coat.

There's salmon
under there!

5. Lay out the foil sheets and divide the vegetables among them. Top each with a salmon fillet . . .

7. Shingle the lemon, lime, and orange slices over each fillet.

6. And spoon the remaining herb mixture on top.

8. Seal the foil parcels by folding the two pieces together and rolling up the ends. Transfer them to a baking sheet. Bake the parcels until the salmon is cooked through and the vegetables are tender, 15 to 17 minutes.

9. Serve the parcels on plates with a side salad and enjoy!

Alex and Bryce. First and third!

TERIYAKI SHRIMP AND PINEAPPLE PARCELS

MAKES 6 SERVINGS

WHAT: Neat foil parcels of delicious "stir-fried" shrimp!

WHEN: When you're ready for your oven to step up and do most of the work.

WHY: Because the flavors are awesome and the cleanup's a cinch!

Foil parcels make me happy. They're just so neat and tidy. You can pack them with virtually any ingredient combination under the sun and feel pretty confident that, after they bake for a bit, they'll wind up holding a steamy, yummy, delicious dinner. Case in point: these cool shrimp and rice parcels. They take on the flavor of a regular stir-fry with two important exceptions: There's no stirring, and there's no frying! But other than that, you'll never know the difference.

2 cups cooked rice

One 8-ounce can pineapple tidbits, drained

1 cup frozen peas

2 red bell peppers, seeded and cut into strips

2 garlic cloves, minced

1½-inch piece fresh ginger, grated

¾ cup thick teriyaki sauce or see page 272

½ teaspoon kosher salt

1½ pounds large shrimp, peeled, deveined, and tails removed

Toasted sesame oil, for drizzling

3 green onions, thinly sliced, for serving

¼ cup chopped cilantro, for serving

1 lime, cut into wedges, for serving

1. Preheat the oven to 450°F. Cut six 12 x 20-inch pieces of foil.

2. Pour the rice into a large bowl and let cool a little.

3. Add the pineapple and peas to the rice . . .

4. Along with the bell peppers, garlic, and ginger.

Who knew you could stir-fry in the oven?

5. Pour in the teriyaki sauce and add the salt . . .

9. Drizzle a tiny amount (about ⅛ teaspoon) of the sesame oil over each parcel

6. And toss the ingredients together until well mixed.

10. Seal the parcels by folding the two pieces together and rolling up the ends.

12. Place a parcel on each plate and carefully open the foil. Add a sprinkle of green onions and cilantro to the top and serve each with a wedge of lime for squeezing.

7. Spoon an equal amount of the rice mixture onto each foil sheet.

11. Place the parcels on a sheet pan and bake for 15 minutes, until the shrimp are opaque.

Eat right out of the foil!

8. Divide the shrimp evenly among the parcels.

Variations

» *Use cooked noodles instead of rice; just precook the noodles for a little less than the required cook time.*

» *Substitute any stir-fry veggies you'd like: diced onions, baby corn, different colors of peppers, quartered white mushrooms, and so forth.*

Instant Pot
Mashed Potatoes
(page 269)

Beef + Lobster =
Ree is happy.

SURF AND TURF SKEWERS

MAKES 2 TO 4 SERVINGS

WHAT: Grilled skewers of succulent lobster and tender beef, served with a spicy hollandaise.

WHEN: Any time you want to wow your special guests.

WHY: Because lobster and tenderloin are M.F.E.O. (made for each other!).

It's a good thing my first introduction to seafood as a child was frozen fish sticks (see page 215), because if it had been grilled chunks of lobster tail, it would have seriously driven up my mom's grocery budget. I can't control myself around lobster; it is my strongest weakness, my one true love, my reason for being. And when it's combined with the king of all beef cuts, tenderloin . . . well, just stick a fork in me because I'm absolutely done. A slightly spicy Cajun-style hollandaise sends these tasty grilled skewers over the top. Make this dinner for someone you seriously want to impress!

1½ teaspoons kosher salt

1 teaspoon smoked paprika

1 teaspoon sweet paprika

½ teaspoon onion powder

½ teaspoon garlic powder

½ teaspoon cayenne pepper

½ teaspoon black pepper

¼ teaspoon ground thyme

Two 4- to 5-ounce raw lobster tails (thawed if you are using frozen)

12 ounces beef tenderloin

3 tablespoons salted butter, melted, for grilling

CAJUN HOLLANDAISE

3 large egg yolks

Juice of ½ lemon

Pinch of kosher salt

1 cup (2 sticks) salted butter, melted (and hot!)

1 tablespoon Creole or other grainy mustard

½ teaspoon cayenne pepper

SAUTÉED KALE

1 tablespoon olive oil

4 cups torn Tuscan kale, stems removed

Kosher salt and black pepper

1. In a small bowl, combine the salt, smoked paprika, sweet paprika, onion powder, garlic powder, cayenne, black pepper, and thyme . . .

3. Next, remove the lobster meat from the tails: Use sharp kitchen shears to cut down both sides of the underside of the tails.

2. Stir the spice rub together and set aside.

4. Grab the end of the outer membrane and peel it backward, exposing the meat underneath . . .

5. And pull the tail meat right out of the shell.

6. Cut both the lobster and the beef into 1-inch chunks.

7. Alternating between steak and lobster, thread the meat onto four 12-inch metal skewers, about 4 pieces of steak and 3 pieces of lobster on each skewer.

8. Sprinkle the spice rub on all sides of the lobster and beef. (You will have a little spice rub left over; it keeps well in a little plastic zipper bag!)

9. Heat a grill pan over medium heat. Meanwhile, make the Cajun hollandaise: In a blender, combine the egg yolks . . .

10. And the lemon juice and salt . . .

11. Then blend on high for 30 seconds, until totally combined.

12. Adjust the blender speed to low and with the machine running, slowly drizzle in the hot melted butter. The sauce will start to get very thick.

This looks perfect!

13. Add the mustard . . .

14. And the cayenne . . .

15. And mix until combined. If it becomes too thick to blend, squeeze in the juice of the other half of the lemon and try again. Put the lid on the blender to keep warm.

16. Grill the skewers, brushing them with melted butter and turning about every minute, until the lobster is cooked through and the steak is rare, 4 to 5 minutes total. Let the skewers rest until you serve them.

17. While the skewers are resting, sauté the kale: Heat a large skillet over medium-high heat and add the olive oil. Cook the kale, sprinkling with salt and pepper to taste, until wilted, about 4 minutes.

18. To serve, place the skewers on a bed of the kale . . .

DID YOU KNOW?

Lobsters live forever! Well, they possibly could—if disease, natural predators, or the market for their deliciousness didn't exist. Lobsters produce telomerase, an enzyme that prevents DNA cells from becoming damaged, which means lobsters could, undisturbed and undiseased, never age—and, yes, live forever. A hefty nineteen-pound lobster was found off the coast of Maine a few years ago, and it was thought to be 140 years old. I'll take some telomerase, please!

19. And pour on that luscious hollandaise.

MISO TILAPIA

MAKES 4 SERVINGS

WHAT: Tender tilapia with a dark, rich sauce.

WHEN: Fish night!

WHY: The marvelousness of miso is massively unmitigated.

I first had black miso fish at a restaurant in New York City approximately a hundred years ago, or maybe it was more like seven. I will never forget that flaky white fish with the striking contrast of the dark, delicious miso. Pure amazement! And while it sure took me a few years, I have finally figured out how to make it at home. This is an incredibly impressive way to prepare fish, and it'll knock your family's (or guests') socks off!

½ cup mirin (sweet Japanese rice wine; you can substitute dry sherry)

¼ cup red miso paste

Juice of 1 lime

1 tablespoon honey

1 teaspoon toasted sesame oil

2 garlic cloves, minced

1 tablespoon grated fresh ginger

Four 6-ounce skinless tilapia fillets, or any other white fish

Sliced green onions, for serving

1. First up: This is a package of red miso, otherwise known as fermented soybeans. Sounds a little unusual, tastes absolutely incredible.

2. In a small bowl, combine the mirin and miso . . .

3. Then throw in the lime juice, honey, sesame oil, garlic, and ginger . . .

4. And use a whisk to vigorously mix the flavorings, trying to remove the larger lumps. (Alternatively, you can use a blender to ensure it's super smooth.)

5. Strain the mixture through a fine-mesh sieve to remove any remaining lumps.

Dark and delicious!

6. Place the tilapia on a foil-lined sheet pan and pour the miso mixture generously over each piece. Chill, uncovered, for at least 1 hour or up to 3 hours.

7. Preheat the oven to 450°F.

8. Bake the fish until it's almost cooked through, about 10 minutes. Switch the oven to broil and broil the fish, another 2 to 3 minutes, watching carefully to ensure it doesn't burn (though you should expect the excess sauce to almost blacken).

9. Serve with the sliced green onions on top.

Lucy Girl loves Walter.
(He sometimes feels
the same way.)

Meatless

Former vegetarian here! You heard me right. When I was in college and a few years beyond, I ate zero meat. (I love regaling my cattle-ranching husband with stories of my experiences!) And even though I can't see myself ever going back to that eating existence full-time, I still love the flavors and creativity that meatless cooking can usher in. The recipes you're about to read are just right on those days that you're A-okay without a main protein. (Once or twice a week is about my speed!)

STREET CORN SOUP

MAKES 8 SERVINGS

WHAT: A hearty Tex-Mex corn chowder.

WHEN: Cold weather or warm! This soup is perfect every day.

WHY: The texture of the soup is delightful, and the fixins make it extra fun!

This is a thick (but not too thick), spicy (but not too spicy), and creamy (but not too creamy) corn soup that's as great for a weeknight dinner as it is for a weekend gathering with good friends. Lay out the soup and fixins and let everyone serve themselves. It's a fun, fabulous soup!

1. Heat a grill pan over medium-high heat. Rub the corn with 2 tablespoons of the olive oil and grill it, turning occasionally, until starting to blacken, about 7 minutes.

3. In a Dutch oven, heat the remaining 2 tablespoons olive oil and the butter over medium heat. Add the onion, jalapeño, poblano, garlic, oregano, chili powder, cumin, salt, and black pepper . . .

2. Remove the corn and let it cool slightly, then use a sharp knife to shave the kernels off the cobs. I like to hold the cobs over a Bundt pan to avoid making a mess!

4. And sauté until the onions have started to soften, about 5 minutes.

8 ears of corn, shucked

4 tablespoons olive oil

2 tablespoons salted butter

1 large yellow onion, diced

1 jalapeño, diced

1 poblano pepper, seeded and diced

5 garlic cloves, minced

2 tablespoons chopped fresh oregano leaves

1 tablespoon chili powder

2 teaspoons ground cumin

1 teaspoon kosher salt

½ teaspoon black pepper

⅓ cup mezcal or tequila (or veggie stock)

4 cups (1 quart) vegetable stock

Juice of 1 lime

¼ cup heavy cream

½ cup grated pepper Jack cheese

FIXINS

Cotija cheese, crumbled

Sour cream

Fresh jalapeño slices

Lime wedges

Cilantro leaves

5. Add the corn and cook for 3 minutes more, stirring occasionally.

9. Use an immersion blender to partially puree the soup—8 to 10 pulses. (You don't want to break up all the corn.)

13. Finally, add the pepper Jack and stir until it's melted.

6. Turn off the heat, then add the mezcal . . .

10. Add the lime juice and stir.

14. Serve with crumbled Cotija, sour cream, jalapeño slices, lime wedges, and cilantro.

7. And the vegetable stock.

11. Add the cream . . .

CRAZY CORN FTW!

Street corn, or *elote*, is corn on the cob grilled over an open flame until blackened, then slathered in a mix of mayonnaise, Mexican crema, lime, Cotija cheese, chile powder, and plenty of salt. It's also known as Crazy Corn, for a very good reason: The authentic stuff really is crazy-good. Unforgettable, actually!

8. Turn on the heat and bring to a boil, then reduce the heat to low and simmer for 30 minutes.

12. And stir. Let it heat up for 5 more minutes.

CAULIFLOWER FRIED RICE

MAKES 4 SERVINGS

WHAT: A lower-carb answer to your fried rice dreams.

WHEN: Dinnertime, low-carb time, any time!

WHY: Because the similarity of the cauliflower to actual rice will amaze and astound you!

In recent years, cauliflower has wormed its way up there as one of the most prominent veggie mainstays in my fridge. Part of this is because I've been pleasantly surprised by how inherently tasty it is, and the other part is that I'm becoming fonder of lower-carb recipes when—and *only* when—said recipes don't compromise on texture or flavor. Substituting finely minced raw cauliflower for the rice will allow you to eat a big ol' plate without dreading thirty minutes into the future, when the fried-rice regret usually sets in.

It's a treat, and I promise you'll love it!

1. Working in 2 or 3 batches, place the cauliflower florets in a food processor.

3. Transfer the batches of cauliflower to a bowl as you go.

2. Pulse several times, until the mixture resembles snow!

4. In a large skillet, heat the vegetable and sesame oils over medium heat. Add the garlic, ginger, and two-thirds of the green onions and cook, stirring constantly, for 1 minute . . .

1 head cauliflower, stem removed, cut into florets

2 tablespoons vegetable oil

1 tablespoon toasted sesame oil

2 garlic cloves, minced

1 tablespoon minced fresh ginger

3 green onions, thinly sliced

3 teaspoons chili paste (sambal oelek), or more to taste

½ cup shredded carrots

2 cups packed baby spinach

3 tablespoons reduced-sodium soy sauce

2 tablespoons salted butter

4 large eggs

2 teaspoons sesame seeds, toasted (see page 80), for serving

Sriracha sauce, for serving

No rice in this fried rice!

5. Then add the chili paste, stir to combine, and cook for another minute.

9. And stir-fry until the cauliflower is tender, 2 to 3 minutes. Add the soy sauce and cook for another minute, until it is absorbed into the cauliflower.

12. Place a generous bed of the "fried rice" on each plate . . .

6. Increase the heat to medium-high and stir in the carrots . . .

10. Stir to make sure the cauliflower is all coated with deliciousness. Remove from the heat and set aside.

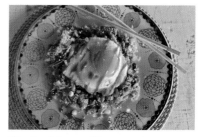

13. And top with an egg. Sprinkle with the sesame seeds and reserved green onions. Add a drizzle of sriracha.

7. Then add the spinach . . .

11. Meanwhile, in a nonstick skillet, melt the butter over medium heat and cook the eggs. For sunny-side up eggs, cook on one side until the whites are almost completely set on top. (Or cook them to your liking.)

8. And the cauliflower rice . . .

Variations

» *Omit the egg and use the cauliflower rice as the foundation for your favorite stir-fry.*

» *Keep the cauliflower rice plain and simple by cooking it in 1 tablespoon butter and seasoning with salt and pepper.*

» *Serve it as a side dish with any main course.*

SWEET POTATO AND KALE TACOS

MAKES 4 TO 6 SERVINGS

WHAT: Veggietastic, meatless (is that redundant?) tacos with a smoky chipotle cream.

WHEN: Meatless Monday or Taco Tuesday! Or Sweet Potato Sunday. Or Cilantro Saturday.

WHY: The colors are rich, the flavor is lush, and they're fun to build and eat!

There are some things I have a hard time eating without meat. Steak, for instance. But with other things, such as these completely yummy veggie tacos, I find myself not missing the meat one bit. They start with roasted sweet potatoes, kale, and red onions, and the rest is taco history! The only thing to watch for is that because the veggies are so good for you, it's hard not to rationalize eating seventeen in one sitting. Or maybe those things only happen to me.

1. Preheat the oven to 450°F.

2. Prepare the veggies: In a bowl, combine the sweet potatoes, kale, and onion. Add the olive oil, melted butter . . .

4. And toss to coat the veggies. Spread the mixture out on a sheet pan.

3. Chili powder, cumin, and salt . . .

5. Roast the veggies, shaking the pan halfway through, until the sweet potatoes are tender and golden and the kale is slightly crisp, about 25 minutes. Set aside covered with foil to keep warm.

VEGGIE TACOS

4 sweet potatoes, peeled and cut into 1-inch cubes

1 bunch curly kale, stems removed, leaves torn into large pieces

½ red onion, thinly sliced

¼ cup olive oil

4 tablespoons (½ stick) butter, melted

2 teaspoons chili powder

½ teaspoon ground cumin

1½ teaspoons kosher salt

12 small corn or flour tortillas

CHIPOTLE CREAM

1 cup sour cream

2 tablespoons adobo sauce from a can of chipotle peppers

Juice of ½ lime

1 teaspoon honey

Kosher salt and black pepper

FOR SERVING

8 ounces Cotija cheese or queso fresco, crumbled

1 cup cilantro leaves

Lime wedges

6. Reduce the oven temperature to 325°F. Wrap the stack of tortillas in the foil and place them in the oven.

10. Place the veggies in a bowl for serving, then remove the tortillas from the oven.

Variations

» *Use butternut squash instead of sweet potatoes.*

» *Add 8 ounces sliced mushrooms to the veggie mixture.*

7. Meanwhile, make the chipotle cream: In a small food processor or blender, combine the sour cream, adobo sauce, lime juice, honey, and a dash each of salt and pepper . . .

11. To serve, pile some of the veggies in the middle of a tortilla . . .

IF NOT TACOS . . .

The sweet potato/kale mixture is so versatile! Eat it on its own or as a side, or try using it in one of these delicious ways:

✿ In quesadillas

✿ On a bowl of brown rice

✿ In nachos

✿ In scrambled egg whites

✿ In pasta

✿ In arugula salad

✿ As a pizza topping

✿ Inside a grilled cheese

✿ Inside a veggie wrap with greens

✿ Tossed in a vinaigrette and chilled for a healthy salad

8. And process until smooth.

9. Transfer the chipotle cream to a bowl for serving.

12. And add a spoonful of chipotle cream and some Cotija crumbles. Top with the cilantro leaves and serve with lime wedges.

EGGPLANT PARMESAN SPAGHETTI SQUASH BOWLS

MAKES 4 SERVINGS

WHAT: Eggplant Parmesan baked in halves of spaghetti squash.

WHEN: When you're ready for a new twist on an Italian classic.

WHY: You won't miss the breading (the eggplant has none) and you won't miss the pasta (the squash is the pasta!).

I understand my hatred of bananas is confounding to some, but by the same token, I am completely baffled by the widespread loathing of eggplant. I think it's a beautiful vegetable, especially when it's topped with marinara and melted cheese (hello, eggplant Parm!). For this meatless (and lower-carb, because it skips the eggplant breading *and* the pasta) marvel, I plunk my favorite eggplant dish into roasted halves of spaghetti squash. I have just seven words left: *Where has this been all my life?!?*

2 medium spaghetti squash, halved lengthwise

Olive oil, for drizzling

Kosher salt and black pepper

1 large eggplant, ends trimmed, cut into 8 rounds

1½ cups jarred marinara sauce, warmed

8 ounces mozzarella cheese, grated (about 2 cups)

¼ cup freshly grated Parmesan cheese, for serving

Torn fresh basil leaves, for serving

1. Position two oven racks in the middle and bottom third of the oven and preheat to 400°F. Line two sheet pans with foil.

2. Using a spoon, scrape the seeds and fibrous strands from the spaghetti squash.

3. Drizzle the cut surfaces of the squash with olive oil and sprinkle generously with salt and pepper.

4. Place the squash cut side down on one of the sheet pans and roast for 40 minutes.

5. Meanwhile, place the eggplant slices on the second sheet pan. Drizzle both sides with olive oil, then sprinkle with salt and pepper. When the spaghetti squash have about 15 minutes left to roast, place the eggplant in the oven.

6. Remove the spaghetti squash from the oven and use a spatula to flip them over. The edges should be very brown.

7. Remove the eggplant from the oven at the same time. Reduce the oven temperature to 350°F.

8. Using a fork, scrape the inside of the squash to loosen the flesh. It looks like spaghetti!

9. Spoon ¼ cup of the marinara on each squash half.

10. Place ¼ cup of the mozzarella on each half.

11. Next, each piece gets two slices of the eggplant . . .

12. 2 more tablespoons marinara . . .

13. And ¼ cup of the remaining mozzarella.

14. Bake until the mozzarella is bubbling, 15 to 17 minutes. Remove the spaghetti squash "bowls" to a platter and sprinkle on the grated Parmesan.

15. Top with torn basil and serve!

MEAN GREEN MAC AND CHEESE

MAKES 8 TO 12 SERVINGS

WHAT: Gloriously green mac and cheese.

WHEN: Dinnertime, lunchtime, Sunday brunch time (and any holiday, too!).

WHY: Because the bright green hue adds a healthy vibe to a dish not exactly known for healthy vibes.

In the past, I have expressed sentiments along the lines of "You could add gravel to mac and cheese and it would still be good," and I stand behind that, even though I wouldn't recommend it. What I *would* recommend is this bright green mac and cheese, made so by the inclusion of greens and herbs. It is truly one of the greatest things I've eaten in the past year, and if you're one of those people who wants to get their daily serving of greens but doesn't necessarily look forward to it, this'll solve that problem!

Butter, for the baking dish

GREENS

3 cups baby spinach

3 cups baby arugula

½ cup fresh basil leaves

⅓ cup fresh mint leaves

¼ cup fresh parsley leaves

2 garlic cloves, peeled

1 teaspoon red pepper flakes

¼ teaspoon kosher salt

¼ teaspoon black pepper

¼ cup olive oil

CHEESE SAUCE

4 tablespoons (½ stick) salted butter

2 tablespoons all-purpose flour

1 teaspoon dry mustard

2 cups whole milk

¼ cup half-and-half

1 teaspoon salt

½ teaspoon black pepper

2 cups grated white Cheddar cheese

2 cups grated Fontina cheese

½ cup grated Monterey Jack cheese

ASSEMBLY

1 pound elbow macaroni, cooked al dente

½ cup panko breadcrumbs

2 tablespoons minced parsley

4 tablespoons (½ stick) salted butter, melted

1. Preheat the oven to 350°F. Butter a 9 x 13-inch baking dish.

2. Prepare the greens: In a food processor, combine the spinach, arugula, basil, mint, parsley, garlic, pepper flakes, salt, and black pepper.

3. Turn on the machine and drizzle in the olive oil . . .

4. But stop while the mixture still has texture. Set aside.

5. Make the cheese sauce: In a large saucepan, melt the butter over medium heat. Sprinkle in the flour and dry mustard and whisk to combine. Let the roux cook for a minute or so, whisking constantly, until it starts to turn golden.

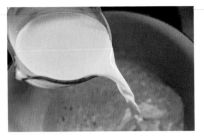

6. Pour in the milk and half-and-half, whisking constantly. Add the salt and pepper . . .

7. And cook, whisking often, until the white sauce is thick and bubbling, about 3 minutes.

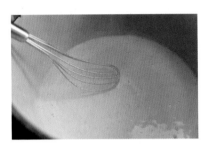

8. Add the Cheddar, Fontina, and Monterey Jack. Stir until the cheese is fully melted.

9. To assemble: Add the cooked macaroni to the cheese sauce and stir, making sure every noodle is coated in sauce.

10. Add the pureed greens and stir until just combined.

11. Pour the pasta mixture into the baking dish and smooth the surface.

12. In a small bowl, combine the panko, parsley, and melted butter and stir.

13. Sprinkle the panko mixture evenly over the surface of the pasta.

14. Bake until bubbling and golden brown, 22 to 25 minutes.

Variation

» *Dice or shred 2 grilled chicken breasts and add them to the mac and cheese for a meatier casserole.*

GREEN IT UP!

You can use the fresh-and-flavorful herb puree to inject gorgeous green color and flavor into dishes like mashed potatoes, scalloped potatoes, fettuccine Alfredo, and risotto! You can also stir it into a regular ranch dressing, or mix it with mayo for a deliciously green sandwich spread. You'll fall in love with the flavor!

CURRIED CAULIFLOWER

MAKES 4 TO 6 SERVINGS

WHAT: Curry-roasted cauliflower with a tangy-sweet golden raisin relish!

WHEN: At dinnertime, as a meatless meal with a side salad.

WHY: Because if cauliflower is king, curry is his crown. I totally just made that up in three seconds, so don't hold it against me.

I haven't been keeping a tally, but if my calculations are correct, this is the third recipe involving cauliflower in this cookbook. So I think we can all agree that I'm enamored of the stuff. Cauliflower's versatility continually fills me with awe, particularly in a dish like this, where it seems to take on a whole new identity. This veggie dish is gloriously golden, fantastically flavorful, and will wake up your dinner table in the most wonderful way. And with that, my alliteration quota for the month has been met.

2 heads cauliflower, stems removed, cut into florets

½ cup olive oil

1 tablespoon curry powder

½ teaspoon kosher salt, plus more for seasoning

½ teaspoon black pepper

2 tablespoons pine nuts

¼ cup red wine vinegar

1½ tablespoons honey

½ cup golden raisins

2 tablespoons chopped cilantro, for serving

1. Preheat the oven to 450°F.

2. In a large bowl, toss the cauliflower, ¼ cup of the olive oil, the curry powder, salt, and pepper.

3. Spread the cauliflower onto a sheet pan and roast for 10 minutes.

4. Remove the pan from the oven, give the cauliflower a toss, and return the pan to the oven. Roast until the edges are starting to brown, another 10 minutes.

Fantastically flavorful!

5. Meanwhile, in a dry skillet, toast the pine nuts over medium heat, tossing occasionally, until they turn slightly golden, about 2 minutes.

7. Increase the heat to medium-high and bring the mixture to a gentle boil. Let it bubble and thicken for another 1 to 2 minutes.

9. Transfer to a platter and garnish with the cilantro.

6. Add the remaining ¼ cup olive oil, the vinegar, honey, and raisins.

8. Pour the mixture over the cauliflower, tossing to coat. Taste and add more salt if needed.

Variations

» *Serve on a bed of arugula for a darn gorgeous salad.*

» *Toss with cooked noodles for a beautiful pasta dish.*

Paige, Todd, and Mr. Photobomber

GRILLED HALLOUMI AND VEGETABLES

MAKES 2 SERVINGS

WHAT: Grilled "squeaky cheese" with gorgeous grilled veggies.

WHEN: When you want to be able to say, "I ate grilled cheese for dinner, and I don't mean the sandwich."

WHY: Because Halloumi is a really unique cheese—and a great source of protein.

First, I need to confess that, until about a year ago, I had never heard of Halloumi, so if you're sitting here wondering what the heck it is, don't worry! Halloumi is a sheep's (and goat's) milk cheese made in the island country of Cyprus. But in layman's terms, Halloumi is a delightfully briny and firm cheese that squeaks between your teeth as you eat it, which makes it a whole lot of fun. The firmness of Halloumi is the key: It means you can actually put it on the grill and color it up with grill marks before the cheese becomes overly soft or melted. It has a lot of protein, so if you're wanting to skip the meat for a meal here and there, it's a great stand-in! A note: Because of high demand and the fact that Cyprus is the primary place Halloumi is made, it can be a bit pricey. But the good news is that it doesn't take a very big piece to make a statement!

(On a separate note, sometimes I call Ladd "Halloumi" instead of "Honey," just to make sure he's paying attention. Try it with your sweetheart sometime!)

Olive oil, for grilling

One 8-ounce block Halloumi cheese, halved horizontally into 2 slabs

5 grape or cherry tomatoes, threaded on a wooden skewer that's been soaked in water for 30 minutes

1 small eggplant, cut lengthwise into 8 wedges

1 orange bell pepper, cut vertically into about 4 slabs

1 zucchini, cut on a diagonal into slabs

3 whole Tuscan kale leaves

Kosher salt and black pepper

1 lemon, halved

2 tablespoons chopped oregano leaves, for serving

1. Brush olive oil on a grill pan and heat it over medium heat.

2. Place the Halloumi and vegetables on a sheet pan. Brush them all generously with olive oil.

3. Pay special attention to the kale leaves: Be sure to brush both sides!

4. Sprinkle the cheese and vegetables with salt and pepper.

5. Place the tomatoes, zucchini, bell pepper, and eggplant on the grill pan . . .

6. And grill them on both sides until tender and slightly charred, about 3 minutes per side. Remove them to a clean sheet pan or a platter.

7. Add the kale leaves to the grill pan, top side down, and grill them for about 1½ minutes. Remove them from the grill pan and add to the other veggies.

8. Finally, brush the pan with oil again and grill the Halloumi and lemon halves, cut side down. Cook the cheese until great grill marks form, about 2 minutes per side.

9. Look at all this loveliness!

10. Arrange the veggies in a serving bowl with the Halloumi. Squeeze the juice of one lemon half over the top and serve with the second lemon half. Sprinkle with the oregano and share with a buddy!

FAJITA VEGGIE ZUCCHINI BOATS

MAKES 4 TO 6 SERVINGS

WHAT: Baked zucchini halves filled with Tex-Mex–style veggies and melted cheese.

WHEN: When you're in the mood for a tasty meatless meal!

WHY: The combination of the zesty cooked veggies and the melted cheese is divine, and a zucchini boat makes the perfect vessel.

Zucchini boats are an amazing lower-carb dish, and they introduce all kinds of delicious possibilities. You can fill/top a halved zucchini with anything you can possibly think of: pizza toppings, taco meat, even chili! My recent favorite, though, has a meatless spin: fajita-seasoned vegetables cooked over high heat and piled into the zucchini with melted cheese. A little salsa, sour cream, and cilantro are the perfect finish. You won't miss the meat!

ZUCCHINI BOATS

3 medium zucchini

Kosher salt and black pepper

2 tablespoons olive oil, plus more for the sheet pan

2 tablespoons salted butter

1 small yellow onion, chopped

2 garlic cloves, minced

1 red bell pepper, seeded and diced

1 yellow bell pepper, seeded and diced

1 orange bell pepper, seeded and diced

4 ounces white button mushrooms, sliced

1 teaspoon chili powder

1 teaspoon ground cumin

⅛ teaspoon cayenne pepper

1 cup grated pepper Jack cheese

TOPPINGS

Salsa

Sour cream

Cilantro leaves

---

1. Preheat the oven to 375°F.

2. Make the zucchini boats: Cut the ends off the zucchini, then slice them in half lengthwise. Use a spoon to scoop out the seeds. Sprinkle the boats with salt and pepper and set them cut side up on a lightly oiled sheet pan.

3. Heat a large skillet over medium-high heat and add the olive oil and butter. When the butter is melted, add the onion, garlic, bell peppers, mushrooms, chili powder, cumin, and cayenne . . .

4. And cook, stirring, until the veggies are soft and starting to brown, about 5 minutes. Season with salt and pepper.

5. Divide the veggies among the zucchini boats . . .

6. Then sprinkle with the pepper Jack.

7. Bake until the cheese has melted and is starting to brown, 12 to 13 minutes.

8. To serve, spoon a little salsa in the middle, then add a dollop of sour cream and cilantro leaves. Serve hot.

DRUNKEN SPAGHETTI

MAKES 6 TO 8 SERVINGS

WHAT: Pasta cooked in red wine (you heard me) and tossed with balsamic mushrooms.

WHEN: When you want to impress your guests, or just curl up and watch a movie with a bowl of purple pasta.

WHY: Because, this is not an exaggeration, my life has never been the same since I tasted this.

I never knew drunken pasta existed before about a year ago, and when I first tried it, it was such a profound and earth-shattering experience that I just stood over the pan (Yes, I was eating it out of the pan. Yes, I was standing up. Yes, I'm weird), unable to have a rational thought. If you love wine, and if you love mushrooms, and I know you love pasta even if you say you don't, you will go absolutely bonkers over this super-simple supper.

3 tablespoons olive oil

4 tablespoons (½ stick) salted butter

1 pound baby bella (cremini) mushrooms, thinly sliced

1 pound white button mushrooms, thinly sliced

Kosher salt and black pepper

1 tablespoon balsamic vinegar

1 pound spaghetti

2 garlic cloves, minced

¼ teaspoon red pepper flakes

1 bottle red wine, such as Chianti

12 fresh basil leaves, torn, for serving

½ cup grated Pecorino-Romano cheese, for serving

1. In a large skillet, heat 2 tablespoons of the olive oil and 2 tablespoons of the butter over medium heat. Add the mushrooms, ¼ teaspoon salt, and ¼ teaspoon pepper . . .

2. And stir and cook . . .

3. Until the mushrooms have cooked down and given off liquid, about 5 minutes. Pour in the vinegar, reduce the heat to low . . .

4. And cook until most of the liquid has reduced. Remove from the heat and set aside.

5. Bring a large pot of lightly salted water to a boil, add the spaghetti, and cook for no more than 3 minutes.

6. Drain the pasta and rinse with cold water to stop the cooking process. Set aside.

7. In the pasta cooking pot, heat the remaining 1 tablespoon olive oil and 1 tablespoon of the butter over medium-low heat. Add the garlic and pepper flakes . . .

8. And stir and cook for 2 minutes.

9. Turn off the burner and add ½ teaspoon salt and the wine. Turn the heat to medium-high and bring the wine to a boil.

10. Add the cooled pasta to the wine, reduce the heat to medium, and cook until the wine is completely absorbed by the pasta, about 5 minutes.

11. Look at that gorgeous purple! Turn off the heat and add the remaining 1 tablespoon butter . . .

12. And the cooked mushrooms. Toss everything together.

13. Tip the pasta and mushrooms onto a platter . . .

14. Add the torn basil leaves over the top . . .

15. And serve with a sprinkling of Pecorino-Romano.

Dig in! You are in for a serious treat.

KUNG PAO CAULIFLOWER

MAKES 2 TO 4 SERVINGS

WHAT: A meat-free version of my favorite Chinese takeout dish.

WHEN: Meatless Monday, or whenever your produce drawer is overrun with cauliflower.

WHY: Because the sauce is so flavorful and the veggies so good, you won't even miss the chicken.

Kung Pao Chicken is my go-to takeout dish whenever I pass by a Chinese restaurant. It's so spicy and flavorful, and if my brow isn't sweating when I finish it, I'm not happy. In my quest to discover a thousand new ways to use cauliflower this year, I turned my beloved stir-fry dish into a meatless wonder, and it's the perfect dinner whenever Ladd and the boys are gone for dinner. And I guess I could make it when they *are* home for dinner. I'd just have to throw a big steak on top. (Hey . . . that wouldn't be half bad!)

SAUCE

⅓ cup reduced-sodium soy sauce

2 tablespoons rice vinegar

1 tablespoon honey

1 tablespoon chili paste (sambal oelek), or more to taste

3 garlic cloves, minced

Grated zest and juice of 1 lime

1 tablespoon grated fresh ginger

1 teaspoon sesame oil

STIR-FRY

1½ tablespoons cornstarch

3 tablespoons peanut oil

1 head cauliflower, stem removed, cut into small florets

1 red bell pepper, seeded and diced

1 green bell pepper, seeded and diced

1 zucchini, cut into small dice

6 small dried hot chile peppers (sold in the Asian foods aisle)

6 green onions, sliced

½ cup unsalted peanuts

1. First, make the sauce: In a small pitcher, mix all the ingredients. Set aside.

3. In a large cast-iron skillet, heat the peanut oil over medium-high heat. Add the cauliflower and cook, stirring, for about 30 seconds.

2. For the stir-fry: In a separate pitcher, lightly whisk the cornstarch and ½ cup water with a fork to make a slurry. Set aside with the sauce.

4. Add the bell peppers and stir and cook for another 30 seconds.

5. Add the zucchini, chile peppers, and half of the green onions . . .

6. And cook, stirring, until the cauliflower has softened slightly and begins to char, about 4 minutes.

7. Pour in the sauce . . .

8. And the slurry along with an additional ½ cup water . . .

9. Then reduce the heat to low and cook, stirring constantly, until the sauce is thick and the veggies are coated, about 1 minute. They should be cooked through but not mushy at all. Add another splash of water if the sauce is too thick.

10. Add the peanuts . . .

11. And toss to coat. Taste and add more chile paste if you like things spicier.

12. Serve with the rest of the green onions sprinkled on top. (Avoid eating the chile peppers, as they are fiery hot!)

Walter likes a good nap after every meal. (Don't we all?)

Learning the ropes!

Sides

My go-to side these days is a big bowl of mixed greens (arugula, spinach, baby kale) with a little olive oil and vinegar. Side dishes don't get any more simple and sublime than that! But if you're wanting to augment your easy side salads, these recipes will fit in nicely with whatever else your dinner plate has going on! There's a mix of starches and veggies, homemade sauces and shortcut methods. Now that's what you call a bright side!

They're fun to smash!

SMASHED CUCUMBER SALAD

MAKES 6 SERVINGS

WHAT: Cold, crisp cucumber pieces with a tasty dressing.

WHEN: Whenever you need a cool, refreshing side! They're great with spicy Asian food.

WHY: Because if you've never smashed a cucumber before, you're about to have some fun.

I started hearing about smashed cucumbers within the last year, when the classic Chinese side dish became ultra trendy in New York. Not that I'm normally up to speed with what is ultra trendy in New York; I'm not that cool. But I do know some cool people, and they educated me about this super-amazing dish, which I'm now incredibly fond of. Before tossing cucumber pieces—and they're rough and rustic pieces, not neatly sliced coins!—in a delicious dressing, you smash them with a rolling pin to make them more receptive to the moisture-draining properties of salt as well as to the flavors of the dressing. This can pass as a side or a snack; or if you add some grilled shrimp or salmon, a complete meal!

1 pound English cucumbers (about 2 cucumbers)

1 tablespoon kosher salt

2 tablespoons olive oil

2 tablespoons fresh lime juice

1 tablespoon packed brown sugar

1 tablespoon grated fresh ginger

1 garlic clove, minced

1 tablespoon toasted sesame oil

1 teaspoon red pepper flakes, plus more (optional) for serving

2 green onions, sliced

Sesame seeds, for serving

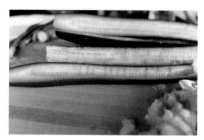  

1. Slice off the ends of the cucumbers, slice them in half lengthwise, and use a spoon to scrape out the seeds.

2. Now this is where it gets fun! Turn the halves cut side down and use a rolling pin to whack them all a couple of times. You want to break and flatten them but not completely tear them apart.

3. This right here is a smashed cucumber!

4. Break each half into 3 or 4 pieces with your hands. You want irregular, jagged pieces!

5. Sprinkle them with the salt, tossing them as you go to coat.

6. Place the cucumbers in a colander and put the colander in a bowl. Let them sit for 12 minutes to drain.

7. Meanwhile, make the dressing: In a small jar, combine the olive oil, lime juice, brown sugar, ginger, garlic, sesame oil, pepper flakes, and half of the green onions. Cover and shake to combine.

8. By now, the cucumbers should have given off liquid, which will make them crisper! Discard the liquid and rinse the bowl.

9. Place the cucumbers in the bowl and pour the dressing on top. Toss to combine.

CHANGE IT UP!

Toss the smashed, salted cucumbers in a creamy dressing instead: Whisk together ½ cup sour cream, 2 teaspoons distilled white vinegar, ½ teaspoon sugar, 2 teaspoons minced fresh dill, and a pinch of salt and pepper. Add to the cucumbers along with some sliced red onion, then fold gently until the cucumbers are coated. Fresh, mild, and tasty!

10. Serve the cucumbers with the remaining green onions and some sesame seeds. If desired, sprinkle with more pepper flakes.

INSTANT POT MASHED POTATOES

MAKES 10 SERVINGS

WHAT: No-drain mashed potatoes that take minutes to make.

WHEN: Side for dinner, or any time you need fuss-free mashed potatoes. (Thanksgiving, anyone?!?)

WHY: Because this takes the hassle out of yer taters. Big-time.

Making mashed potatoes in my Instant Pot has been a godsend! Gone are the days of plopping potatoes in boiling water and having to check their tenderness with a fork until I finally deem them done. In this method, the Instant Pot checks their tenderness with a fork! And actually, it doesn't have to, because it already knows they'll be perfect. The fact that there's no draining required is the icing on the ca . . . I mean the butter on the mashed potatoes!

5 pounds Yukon Gold potatoes, peeled and quartered

2½ teaspoons kosher salt, plus more to taste

1 cup (2 sticks) salted butter, plus more for serving

12 ounces cream cheese

½ cup half-and-half

½ cup heavy cream

½ teaspoon seasoned salt, such as Lawry's

1 teaspoon black pepper, plus more for serving

1. Place the potatoes in the Instant Pot.

3. Secure the lid and set the pressure valve to Sealing. Press the Manual button and set to 10 minutes. (Note that it will take some time for the pressure to build up; from there the 10-minute clock begins!)

5. When the pressure is released (you'll see the button pop down), remove the lid. There should be very little (if any) water on the bottom; if there is any, remove the pot and drain the water off.

2. Add 1½ cups water and 1 teaspoon of the kosher salt.

4. When the cook time is up, use a wooden spoon to move the valve to Venting to let the pressure release quickly.

6. Mash the potatoes, letting as much steam escape as possible.

7. Add the butter, cream cheese, half-and-half, heavy cream, seasoned salt, remaining 1½ teaspoons kosher salt, and the pepper . . .

8. And stir until everything is melted and combined. Taste and adjust the seasonings as needed.

9. Transfer the potatoes to a serving dish, sprinkle with extra black pepper, and top with a few pats of butter.

MY FAVORITE POTATOES!

Red

Quartered or diced in stews and soups or boiled and smashed (skin and all!) with butter, salt, and pepper.

Yellow

Slightly sweet and firm, these golden beauties make the greatest potato salad. They hold together well and never get mealy or mushy!

Baby Yellow

Mild and sweet! I boil them whole until tender, then throw them in a skillet with butter, minced garlic, and minced parsley and sauté them until crisp.

Baby Red "Creamer" Potatoes

Incredibly versatile, these cute little wonders are bred to be small and can be microwaved, boiled, or pan-fried. Always soft and tender!

Russet

The workhorse of the potato world! My go-to for mashed potatoes because of their light, fluffy texture. (Also my go-to for French fries!)

TERIYAKI GRILLED VEGETABLES

MAKES 4 TO 6 SERVINGS

WHAT: Terrifically tasty grilled vegetables marinated in homemade teriyaki sauce.

WHEN: When you need a beautiful side for chicken, steak, fish, or pork.

WHY: Because vegetables were meant to be grilled. Like, totally!

I've loved grilled vegetables since 1993. I know this because in 1993 I attended the wedding of some friends of mine in California, and at the outdoor afternoon reception, on a beautiful buffet table draped with tulle, there sat silver platter after silver platter of mouthwatering wedding reception food. But it wasn't the prime rib or the pork tenderloin or the roasted chicken that captured my attention. I know this because I was a vegetarian at the time. But also, what really stole my heart on that buffet table was an enormous, overflowing platter of grilled vegetables of every kind. It was a feast for the senses, and I've never forgotten how good they tasted! I've been grilling vegetables ever since, and I've found that with a from-scratch teriyaki sauce, they're even more irresistible.

TERIYAKI SAUCE

1 cup reduced-sodium soy sauce

½ cup packed brown sugar

½ cup honey

¼ cup seasoned rice vinegar

¼ cup vegetable oil

2 tablespoons chili paste (sambal oelek)

1 tablespoon grated fresh ginger

1 tablespoon toasted sesame oil

1 tablespoon hot chili oil

1 teaspoon black pepper

4 green onions, sliced

2 garlic cloves, minced

Juice of 1 large lime

VEGETABLES

2 medium zucchini, ends cut off, quartered lengthwise

2 small yellow squash, ends cut off, quartered lengthwise

1 red bell pepper, seeded and cut into large chunks

1 green bell pepper, seeded and cut into large chunks

1 small bunch asparagus, ends trimmed

1 large yellow onion, cut into rounds

Sesame seeds, for serving

Sliced green onions, for serving

1. First, make the teriyaki sauce: In a medium saucepan, combine all the ingredients . . .

2. And whisk until well combined.

3. Place the pan over medium-high heat and bring to a boil. Reduce the heat to medium-low and let simmer gently for 10 minutes. Set aside to cool slightly.

5. And toss the vegetables until well coated in the sauce (add a little more if they need it!) and let them sit for 10 minutes.

7. When the veggies are tender with lots of blackened areas (2 to 3 minutes per side), remove them from the grill.

4. Prepare the veggies: In a large bowl, combine the zucchini, squash, bell peppers, asparagus, and onion rounds. Drizzle ⅔ cup of the teriyaki sauce on top . . .

6. Heat a grill or grill pan over medium-high heat. Grill the vegetables in batches, basting with extra sauce while they cook.

8. Serve with your favorite protein, with sesame seeds and green onions sprinkled on top. Add extra sauce if you like!

I'll take a side dish of sunrise, please!

Variations

» *Add halved mushrooms, eggplant slices, yellow or orange bell pepper wedges, whole green onions, or any other vegetable you'd like.*

» *For an obvious time-saver, use good-quality store-bought teriyaki sauce!*

CHEESY ITALIAN BREAD STICKS

MAKES 12 BREAD STICKS

WHAT: Soft and chewy puff pastry twists bursting with cheese and herbs.

WHEN: Predinner appetizer, dinnertime side, accompaniment to salad, party munchie.

WHY: Because cheese and bread are essential to a happy life.

I never know whether to call these delights bread sticks, cheese sticks, cheese straws, bread twists, cheesy bread straws, bread stick cheese straws, or cheese straw bread stick twists. And now that I have totally worn out your eyes with those options, allow me to share this simply perfect recipe for some of the most delectable little sticks of bread on earth. You'll never run out of reasons or occasions to make them . . . which is not necessarily a good thing. They're habit forming!

1 sheet frozen puff pastry, thawed in the fridge overnight

Flour, for sprinkling

2 tablespoons salted butter, melted

1 cup grated mozzarella cheese (the firmer "supermarket" kind rather than fresh)

¾ cup grated Parmesan cheese

2 tablespoons chopped fresh oregano leaves

1 tablespoon chopped fresh basil leaves

1 large egg

Warm marinara sauce, for serving

1. Preheat the oven to 400°F. Line a baking sheet with parchment paper.

2. Remove the puff pastry from the package and unfold it. Lightly flour a large cutting board and use a rolling pin to slightly roll it out and flatten it a bit.

3. Brush the entire surface with the melted butter . . .

4. Then sprinkle the mozzarella, ½ cup of the Parmesan, and the herbs evenly over the top so that they completely cover the pastry.

5. Roll over the surface with the rolling pin, pressing lightly to anchor the cheeses and herbs.

6. Cut the pastry lengthwise into 12 strips. (A pizza cutter works nicely!)

7. Then, starting in the center of a strip, begin twisting in opposite directions until you reach the ends, creating a spiral.

10. Brush the bread sticks with the egg wash . . .

13. Let the bread sticks sit for 10 minutes, then remove them from the pan.

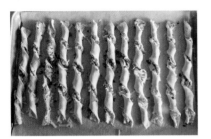

8. Transfer the twists to the prepared baking sheet and freeze for 20 minutes.

11. And sprinkle the tops with the remaining ¼ cup Parmesan.

14. Serve them warm or at room temperature with warm marinara sauce.

9. Meanwhile, in a small bowl, use a fork to mix the egg with 1 tablespoon water.

12. Bake until golden brown, 10 to 11 minutes.

Variations

» *Use grated Cheddar and finely diced jarred jalapeños for a different flavor combination.*

» *Turn them into pizza bread sticks by sprinkling finely minced pepperoni over the cheese before cutting and twisting.*

» *Make the bread sticks smaller by cutting them in half after removing them from the freezer.*

CLASSIC COLLARD GREENS

MAKES 8 SERVINGS

WHAT: Slow-simmered collards with onion, garlic, and ham hock.

WHEN: As a side for pork chops, fried chicken, meatloaf, mac and cheese, black-eyed peas, or ribs!

WHY: Collards have stood the test of time for a reason. They're hearty (and they're darn good for you!).

Collard greens were not a huge part of my mom's cooking when I was growing up, since Oklahoma is not really a Southern state by culinary standards. But through the years, their dark green, delicious mysteriousness has found its way to my table more and more. I love that you can cook them and cook them and they still hold themselves together—and that they seem to absorb the flavors of the ingredients you cook them with. Try to include them on your table more in the coming year. It'll be a leafy green adventure!

2 tablespoons olive oil

1 yellow onion, halved and thinly sliced

5 garlic cloves, minced

2½ cups chicken broth

1 ham hock

3 large bunches collard greens, stems removed, rinsed clean and chopped

2 tablespoons apple cider vinegar

Kosher salt and black pepper

1. In a large Dutch oven, heat the olive oil over medium heat. Add the onion and garlic and sauté until the onion is translucent, 2 to 3 minutes.

3. Then pile the collards on top. The pot will be crowded, but continue to stir until the greens have cooked down into the liquid a bit, about 5 minutes.

5. Until the greens are soft, about 1 hour.

2. Add the broth and ham hock . . .

4. Reduce the heat to low, cover the pot, and simmer . . .

6. Add the vinegar, then stir, taste, and add salt and pepper as needed. (If it is a meaty ham hock, you can use a fork to pull some of the meat off the bone and stir it in!)

ROASTED POTATOES WITH SAGE

MAKES 6 SERVINGS

WHAT: Crispy, oven-fried wedges of buttery, sage-seasoned potatoes.

WHEN: As a side for any steak or roast beef dinner (or salad dinner!).

WHY: Because slow-roasted taters are always worth the time.

Roasted potatoes are such a common side dish that I almost decided not to include them in this cookbook. But then I changed my mind when I woke up and realized that these roasted potatoes are so sensationally sizzle-y and buttery, they're effectively French fries masquerading as something upscale and elegant. Sign me up!

2½ pounds Yukon Gold potatoes, scrubbed clean

4 tablespoons (½ stick) salted butter

¼ cup olive oil

4 garlic cloves, minced

12 fresh sage leaves, minced, plus small leaves for serving

1 teaspoon kosher salt

1 teaspoon black pepper

1. Preheat the oven to 425°F.

2. Cut the potatoes into quarters and set them aside.

4. And stir until the garlic is fragrant, about 1 minute. Remove from the heat.

6. Carefully remove the pan from the oven and stir the potatoes with a wooden or metal spoon. Return the pan to the oven and roast . . .

3. In a large cast-iron skillet, melt the butter in the olive oil over medium heat. Add the garlic and sage . . .

5. Add the potatoes to the skillet and toss. Sprinkle with the salt and pepper, toss again, and place the skillet in the oven for 20 minutes.

7. Until the potatoes are tender and crisp, about 20 minutes. Toss to make sure all the potatoes are coated and sizzling. Garnish with sage leaves and serve.

PERFECT POTATO PARCELS

MAKES 4 SERVINGS

WHAT: Tender foil-baked potato chunks with a buttery, creamy sauce.

WHEN: An easy side for grilled chicken, steak, or fish.

WHY: Because they're baked in the same vessel they're served in, and there's no cleanup after!

I'm always thinking of different ways to cook russet potatoes, but I'd say this method wins the prize in terms of ease of preparation and cleanup. Generous chunks of taters are baked snug inside foil packs with a little onion, garlic, butter, and cream . . . and the resulting side is wonderful. They take on a casual camp-out feel, but you don't have to pitch a tent to enjoy them. This will become a favorite at your dinner table!

3 russet potatoes, scrubbed clean and cut into large chunks	3 garlic cloves, minced	4 tablespoons (½ stick) salted butter
1 yellow onion, cut into large chunks	Kosher salt and black pepper	¼ cup heavy cream
	Smoked paprika	Minced fresh parsley, for serving

1. Preheat the oven to 375°F. Prepare four 12-inch squares of foil.

2. In a large bowl, toss together the potatoes, onion, and garlic.

3. Divide the potatoes and onion among the four foil squares. Sprinkle with salt, pepper, and smoked paprika.

4. Place 1 tablespoon of the butter on each pile. Splash on some of the cream.

5. Wrap the bundles tightly, set them on a sheet pan, and bake until the potatoes are extremely tender (open up a packet—watch out for the steam!—and test with a skewer), about 45 minutes.

6. Unwrap the bundles and sprinkle the parsley on top. Serve the parcels right on the plate.

Variations

» *Add a sprinkle of Parmesan or Cheddar cheese along with the butter and cream.*

» *Add a splash of dry white wine to each parcel.*

CARROT NOODLES

MAKES 6 TO 8 SERVINGS

WHAT: Thin strips of tricolor carrots roasted and tossed in a glorious thyme-infused honey.

WHEN: Dinner party, Easter brunch, summer lunch.

WHY: These carrots make the most beautiful side dish! Or you can use them as a bed of noodles for your favorite protein or veggie dish.

Most days I can take fruit or leave it (egads—did I just say that out loud?), but I know full well I couldn't subsist very long without vegetables. I crave them like some people crave candy, and before that statement comes across as obnoxiously health-conscious, please keep in mind that the vegetable dish I'm about to share with you is tossed in honey. So, yeah . . . candy, basically. (But carrots are good for your eyes!)

2 pounds carrots in mixed colors (orange/purple/white), peeled

¼ cup olive oil

1 teaspoon kosher salt

½ teaspoon black pepper

⅓ cup honey

1 tablespoon minced fresh thyme leaves

Juice of 1 lemon

1. Preheat the oven to 425°F.

2. With a peeler, peel the carrots into long ribbons, rotating the carrot with each peel.

3. Arrange the carrot strips on two rimmed sheet pans, drizzle on the olive oil, and sprinkle with the salt and pepper. Toss to coat, then roast for 10 minutes.

4. Meanwhile, in a small saucepan, combine the honey, thyme, half the lemon juice, and 1 tablespoon water.

Variations

» *Substitute parsnips for some of the carrots for a different combination of flavors.*

» *Use balsamic vinegar instead of lemon juice in the thyme honey to give it a unique zip.*

5. Set over medium-low heat and heat until the edges begin to bubble, 2 to 3 minutes. Remove from the heat and set aside.

6. When the carrots have roasted 10 minutes, remove them from the oven, drizzle on the thyme honey . . .

7. And toss to coat.

8. Mound the carrots on a serving platter and squeeze the remaining lemon juice over the top.

Cowboy Caleb!

BRYCE'S BROCCOLINI

MAKES 4 SERVINGS

WHAT: A simple-ingredient veggie dish that's a cinch to whip up.

WHEN: Dinnertime! It's one of the greatest sides in the USA, Europe, and South America. Or at least our house on the ranch.

WHY: Because broccolini is deliciously addictive, and you can just taste how healthy it is. Plus, the bright green color seriously makes your plate pretty.

Bryce is my third child—the only baby I gave birth to without the assistance of medication—and has dimples that kill my heart daily. He also happens to be my best eater, and has always inhaled green vegetables like they were Sour Patch Kids. This is Bryce the Dimpled's favorite way to eat broccolini—and it'll immediately be yours, too, once you give it a try. The mixture of butter, lemon, and soy is curiously delectable!

3 tablespoons salted butter

1 pound broccolini

1 lemon

2 tablespoons reduced-sodium soy sauce

Anthony Michael Hall lookalike!

1. In a large nonstick skillet, melt 2 tablespoons of the butter over medium heat. Add the broccolini and toss, cooking it for 1 minute.

3. Add the soy sauce and toss to combine.

5. Then squeeze in the juice of the lemon . . .

2. Grate the lemon zest right into the pan.

4. Add the remaining 1 tablespoon butter . . .

6. And continue tossing and cooking the broccolini until the edges start to brown and the stalks are slightly tender, about 3 minutes.

FOR THE LOVE OF BROCCOLINI

Broccolini is a bit of a mystery. It's easy to assume it is simply "immature" or "baby" broccoli, but that actually isn't the case. It's a hybrid vegetable originally developed in Japan, a cross between regular broccoli and Chinese broccoli, which (confusingly!) is also known as Chinese kale. In everyday eaters' terms, broccolini is everything that's wonderful about regular broccoli, but with long, tender stems, delicious leaves, and almost zero prep time: You just chop off the very bottom and cook it whole. And because of the Chinese broccoli/Chinese kale that's in the mix, there's a unique, almost addictive flavor that sets broccolini apart.

Aside from cooking it in a skillet, my second favorite way to enjoy broccolini is to roast it. Just toss broccolini in olive oil, making sure all the tender ends get coated, and sprinkle it with salt and pepper. Roast it on a sheet pan at 425°F for 13 to 15 minutes, until you see little charred areas . . . and you'll be in Heaven! And here's where the magic happens: You can enjoy the roasted broccolini immediately as a side dish, or you can store it in the fridge and make a beautiful roasted broccolini salad the next day. Just toss the roasted, cold broccolini in a simple vinaigrette and add shaved Parmesan and pine nuts. Bright green broccolini Heaven!

"Gimme some sugar."

Small Sweet Bites

I'm one of those poor souls who have to have a sweet after dinner. I also kind of need a sweet after lunch. A sweet after breakfast wouldn't be bad, either. What I'm saying is, I have a problem. Fortunately, this chapter is the solution! Every sweet bite is small, easy to grab, and big on richness so a little bite goes a long, long way.

CHOCOLATE CHERRY CREAM CHEESE PIE BITES

MAKES 36 TINY PIES

WHAT: Little chocolate/cherry/cream cheese bites.

WHEN: Pretty much for any reason, any day, any moment, any time. These are just lovely!

WHY: Because a 1-inch piece of pie is probably a little better for your waistline than a whole pie.

These darling (and decadent) little sweet treats have all the goodness of a delectable pie in a diminutive package. You will love them . . . over and over and over again!

CRUST

30 Oreos

6 tablespoons (¾ stick) salted butter, melted

FILLING

8 ounces cream cheese, at room temperature

½ cup powdered sugar

1 teaspoon vanilla extract

36 cherries from canned cherry pie filling, with their sauce

4 ounces white chocolate, melted

1. Preheat the oven to 350°F. Line 36 cups of two mini-muffin tins with paper liners.

2. Make the crust: Place the cookies in a food processor . . .

4. Continue pulsing while adding the melted butter . . .

6. Add mounded tablespoons of the crumbs to each cup and use your fingers to pack them firm and make a well (see page 297).

3. And pulse them until they're totally broken up into fine crumbs.

5. Until the mixture is very moist.

7. Bake the crusts for 8 minutes. If the crusts have lost their shape, use the handle of a wooden spoon to reshape them a bit. Let them cool completely.

8. When the crusts are cool, make the filling: In the bowl of a stand mixer fitted with the paddle attachment, combine the cream cheese, powdered sugar, and vanilla . . .

9. And beat the mixture until smooth, scraping the sides of the bowl halfway through, about 3 minutes.

10. Add about 1 teaspoon of the filling to each of the cooled crusts.

11. Top each with a cherry (with a little sauce).

12. Use a small spoon to drizzle the melted white chocolate back and forth over each pie. Place the pans in the fridge to set the chocolate completely.

13. Serve them at a party, or store them in the fridge and eat them as the craving strikes!

They're seriously irresistible.

KEY LIME PIE BITES

MAKES 36 TINY PIES

WHAT: Cute (and crave-worthy) mini Key lime pies

WHEN: When you need a teeny, tangy taste!

WHY: Because one of these will keep you from wanting a big slice of pie. Theoretically . . .

I am totally into mini pies these days. First of all, they don't take as long to bake. Second, they stay nice and neat, as you don't have to mess with the constant slicing of a pie. Third, and most important, they give you a pie fix and keep you from wanting a larger piece. These cute little Key lime babies will rock your world!

CRUST

18 graham crackers (the large rectangles)

2 heaping tablespoons grated lime zest

⅓ cup sugar

12 tablespoons (1½ sticks) salted butter, melted

FILLING

1 heaping tablespoon grated lime zest, plus more for garnish

½ cup fresh lime juice

2 large egg yolks

One 14-ounce can sweetened condensed milk

Whipped cream, for serving (optional)

1. Preheat the oven to 350°F. Line 36 cups of two mini-muffin tins with paper liners.

2. Make the crust: Place the graham crackers in a food processor, breaking them up as you go.

4. Add the lime zest and sugar.

6. Until the crumbs are very moist. You should want to eat them by the spoon until they're gone! But don't.

3. Pulse them several times so that they're mostly broken up into fine crumbs.

5. Continue pulsing while adding the melted butter . . .

7. Add mounded tablespoons of crumbs to each cup.

Key lime luciousness!

8. Use your fingers to pack them firm . . .

9. Then use your finger to make a well in each cup.

10. Bake for 7 minutes, until the crusts start to toast. If they have lost their shape, use the handle of a wooden spoon to reshape them. Let them cool slightly while you make the filling.

11. Make the filling: In a large bowl, combine the lime zest, lime juice, egg yolks, and sweetened condensed milk . . .

12. And whisk until smooth.

13. Fill each cup with 1 generous tablespoon of the mixture.

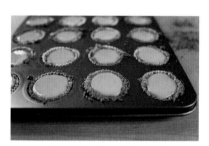

14. Bake until set, 6 to 7 minutes. Refrigerate until completely chilled, at least 2 hours.

15. Sprinkle them with extra lime zest . . .

16. And store them, covered in plastic wrap, in the fridge. Grab one when you have a Key lime craving!

Psst. A little whipped cream is nice, too!

ANIMAL COOKIES

MAKES ABOUT THIRTY 1½-INCH COOKIES

WHAT: Homemade versions of the cute pink animal cookies we all know and love.

WHEN: When you have kids in the house, or when you want to feel like a kid again.

WHY: Once you taste the homemade goodness, you'll see what the store-bought version is missing!

I love those pink-iced animal cookies from the store as much as the next person, but then I decided to make my own, using my mom's age-old sugar cookie recipe as the base. It was then I realized that, while the store-bought cookies are fun and all, there is nothing better than their from-scratch counterparts. These are a blast to make with the kids! (Even if they're big kids, otherwise known as grown-ups.)

DOUGH

10 tablespoons (1¼ sticks) salted butter, softened

¾ cup granulated sugar

½ teaspoon vanilla extract

1 large egg

2 cups all-purpose flour, plus more for dusting

1½ teaspoons baking powder

¼ teaspoon kosher salt

1 tablespoon plus 1 teaspoon whole milk

GLAZE

2 cups powdered sugar

5 drops red food coloring

Rainbow sprinkles

1. Make the dough: In the bowl of a stand mixer fitted with the paddle attachment, cream the butter and sugar, scraping the bowl halfway through.

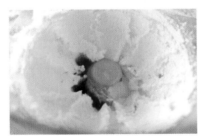

2. Add the vanilla and egg and mix until combined.

3. Sift together the flour, baking powder, and salt into a bowl.

4. With the mixer on low, alternate adding the flour mixture . . .

5. With the milk. You'll want to add one-third of the flour and half the milk in each addition.

6. Stop mixing when the dough just comes together.

7. Flatten the dough into a disc and put it into a plastic bag. Refrigerate until chilled, about 2 hours.

8. Preheat the oven to 350°F. Line two sheet pans with parchment paper or baking mats.

9. On a floured surface, roll out the dough to a ¼-inch thickness.

10. Cut out as many cookies as you can using small animal shapes . . .

11. And place them on the prepared sheet pans.

12. Bake until they're just barely done and golden around the bottom edges, 9 to 10 minutes.

13. Transfer the cookies to two cooling racks and let them cool completely.

14. Make the glaze: Sift the powdered sugar into a bowl. Add ¼ cup water . . .

15. And whisk to combine. Add a tiny bit more water if it's too thick.

16. Add the food coloring . . .

17. And whisk until combined.

18. Drop a cookie upside down in the glaze, pressing until it's halfway submerged.

19. Place it right side up on the cooling rack . . .

20. And immediately add the sprinkles.

The Merc!

22. Let the glaze set completely at room temperature, or place them in the fridge until it sets if you're in a hurry!

21. Continue with all the cookies!

23. Serve them right away, or store them in airtight containers!

ICE CREAM BONBONS

MAKES ABOUT 32 BONBONS

WHAT: Sweet miniature ice cream scoops coated in a homemade chocolate shell.

WHEN: Any time you need a hit of sweetness!

WHY: Because they'll keep you from filling up a bowl with seven scoops of ice cream. Theoretically . . .

Little chocolate-covered ice cream bites like these are both a blessing and a curse. A blessing, because if you have a little sweet tooth attack, you can easily reach into your freezer for a no-fuss fix. A curse, for the same reason. But if you can tell your sweet tooth (or teeth, in my case) to be happy with one (two, max!) satisfied craving a day, you'll really love (and get used to) having these in your freezer. A side bonus of this recipe is that it shows you how to make your own version of the quick-to-harden chocolate shell used for dip cones in classic Tastee-Freez stores. Who knew it was such a cinch?

1½ pints ice cream (pistachio, coffee, chocolate, strawberry, vanilla, and so forth)

2 cups roughly chopped semisweet chocolate

¼ cup coconut oil

¼ cup sprinkles (jimmies, chopped nuts, chopped candies, and so forth)

1. Line a sheet pan with parchment paper. Working quickly, portion out the ice cream using a 1½-tablespoon scoop.

2. Freeze for at least 2 hours; several hours is better!

3. Twenty minutes before you are ready to make the bonbons, in a microwave-safe bowl, combine the chocolate and coconut oil.

4. Heat in the microwave in 30-second increments, stirring after each, until the mixture is melted and smooth. Let cool for 10 minutes, stirring every couple of minutes.

5. When the ice cream scoops are frozen solid and the chocolate mixture has cooled to lukewarm, remove the ice cream scoops from the freezer and lay out fresh parchment on a sheet pan. Place a scoop of ice cream on a fork . . .

6. And dunk it quickly, letting the excess chocolate drip off.

7. Place the scoop on the clean parchment (use a toothpick to help scoot it off the fork).

8. Before the chocolate sets, sprinkle on any topping you'd like!

9. Return the bonbons to the freezer to firm up, about 2 more hours.

10. Transfer to a freezer bag or container and freeze for up to 2 months.

Not . . .

That they . . .

Will last that long.

Have fun filling your freezer with a mix of ice cream flavors and sprinkles. It's my new hobby!

MINI CHURRO BITES

MAKES ABOUT 8 SERVINGS

WHAT: Teeny-tiny churros! Yes, please.

WHEN: Any time you need a sweet snack. Great for a room full of teenagers!

WHY: Because a few small churro bites are better for you than a nine-foot-long churro. (See how I rationalize my life choices?)

I can't think of many things that are more sinfully delightful than churros. Who can argue with a long stick of deep-fried dough, after all, especially if that fried dough is coated in sweet cinnamon sugar and dipped in luscious caramel sauce? I mean . . . c'mon. These are the things that inhabit one's dreams. Here's a way to make churros that are more bite-size, which I love because you don't have to commit to a huge, long churro . . . and they're tailor-made for dipping. The classic method for squeezing churro batter into the hot oil is to use a pastry bag with a large star tip, but if you don't have one, you can use two spoons to simply drop teaspoon-sized clumps of dough into the oil! They'll have more of a doughnut hole shape, but will still be delicious.

Note that they're best within an hour of frying, so gather an eager crowd!

Vegetable oil, for deep-frying	1 tablespoon kosher salt	1½ teaspoons ground cinnamon
½ cup whole milk	1½ cups all-purpose flour	Caramel sauce, store-bought or homemade (see Caramel Apple Quesadillas, page 331), for serving
2 tablespoons unsalted butter	1 teaspoon baking soda	
1 cup plus 2 tablespoons sugar	1 large egg	

1. Pour 2½ inches of vegetable oil into a large cast-iron pot or deep skillet and heat over medium-high heat until a deep-frying thermometer registers 360°F.

2. In a medium saucepan, combine the milk, butter, 2 tablespoons of the sugar, the salt, and 1¼ cups water. Bring to a boil over medium-high heat, then remove from the heat.

3. In a medium bowl, mix together the flour and baking soda.

4. Sprinkle the flour mixture into the saucepan . . .

5. And stir quickly to bring the mixture together. (It gets thick very quickly, so use your muscles!)

6. Add the egg and stir it in until combined. Set the mixture aside to cool slightly.

7. Fill a pastry bag fitted with a large star tip with batter. (Note: It helps to fill the bag with just half of the batter at a time.) Carefully hold the tip close to the oil and squeeze out 1 inch of batter at a time, cutting off the pieces with kitchen shears as you go.

8. Fry in batches of about 12 mini churros at a time, moving them around with a metal spoon or spatula so that they brown evenly. They take only about 1½ minutes to fry to a deep golden brown.

9. Remove them to paper towels to drain as you fry the rest.

10. In a large bowl, stir together the remaining 1 cup sugar and the cinnamon. When the churros are all fried, drop them in batches into the cinnamon sugar, tossing to coat well.

11. Move the churros to more paper towels and give them a final sprinkle of cinnamon sugar before serving.

12. Serve them warm with little cups of caramel sauce!

MINI GLAZED BROWNIES

MAKES ABOUT 60 BITE-SIZE BROWNIES

WHAT: Pop-in-your-mouth brownie bites.

WHEN: Any time you need a rich chocolate fix but you're trying to be good.

WHY: Because sometimes a bite of chocolate is all you need, I think.

I don't understand human beings who don't have to have a sweet bite after a meal. My sister is one of those odd types, and again—I don't get it. These little brownie bites have become one of my favorite things to keep around the kitchen, because they are so rich and delicious, sometimes just one is all I need. And while I guess it could be argued that it's healthier to push away dessert entirely, I'd venture to say that a little bite never hurt anyone! (Except for Snow White. But that's a bedtime story for another time.)

Baking spray

1 cup (2 sticks) salted butter

5 ounces unsweetened chocolate, broken into pieces

¼ cup unsweetened cocoa powder

2 cups sugar

1 tablespoon vanilla extract

3 large eggs

1¼ cups all-purpose flour

½ cup heavy cream

4 ounces bittersweet chocolate, broken into pieces

Chopped pistachios (optional)

Rainbow sprinkles (optional)

Lucy and Paige are BFFs!

1. Preheat the oven to 350°F. Spray a 9 x 13-inch pan with baking spray and line the bottom with parchment paper, leaving 6 inches of overhang of the parchment on the two long sides.

5. And the sugar and stir to combine.

9. Sift in the flour and stir until just barely combined.

2. In a medium saucepan, combine the butter and unsweetened chocolate . . .

6. Add the vanilla . . .

10. Pour the batter into the prepared pan and smooth the surface. Bake until a toothpick inserted in the center comes out clean, 22 to 24 minutes.

3. And stir frequently over low heat until the mixture is fully melted and smooth. Remove it from the heat.

7. And the eggs . . .

11. Let the brownies cool completely in the pan, then use the parchment overhang to lift them out of the pan. Peel back the parchment.

4. Add the cocoa powder . . .

8. And stir until the mixture just comes together.

12. Use a long serrated knife to cut the brownie block into strips, then into small squares. (Trim the ends as needed to keep them evenly sized. The trimmed pieces are a snack in themselves!)

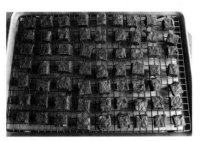

13. Transfer the brownie bites to a rack set over a sheet pan and set them aside.

14. Next, make the ganache! In a small saucepan, heat the cream over medium-high heat until hot but not simmering. Set the bittersweet chocolate in a small heatproof bowl and pour the hot cream over it.

15. Let it sit for 2 minutes, then stir until melted and completely smooth.

16. Transfer the ganache to a squirt bottle and squeeze a little over each brownie, letting it drip over the sides. If you prefer, you can drizzle it on with a small spoon.

17. Before the ganache sets, sprinkle on the pistachios and/or sprinkles, if using!

18. Continue until they're all done, then let the ganache set.

19. Serve them on a platter . . .

20. Or store them in an airtight container for easy snackin'!

Variation

» *Use any toppings you'd like! Chopped toffee, any chopped roasted nuts, any kind of sprinkles!*

He's better than dessert.
(Don't tell dessert I said that.)

Desserts

It all comes down to desserts, doesn't it? I mean, we can discuss all the chicken, beef, and seafood recipes we want . . . but isn't it just pretense when the whole goal, obviously, is getting our hands on dessert? I did some soul-searching about the sweets I would share with you in this chapter. I wanted some surprises, some delights, some familiar faves . . . and I wanted you to look at every recipe and think "Holy, moly. I must make that today." So you'll find a mix of cakes, cookies, frozen desserts, fried doughs, ice creams . . . each one with a healthy dose of Heaven inside. Enjoy these, friends. You deserve it!

BUTTERSCOTCH LAVA CAKES

MAKES 4 SERVINGS

WHAT: The lava cake you know and love—featuring ooey-gooey butterscotch instead of chocolate!

WHEN: Any time you're in the mood for a luscious little cake on a plate.

WHY: Because they're very fast to pull together, and because they're 100 percent unforgettable.

I'm always hesitant to declare any one recipe in a cookbook my favorite, because let's face it—they're all my favorites or they wouldn't have made the cut. Also, I wouldn't want you to look at the other hundred-plus recipes in this book and think, "This one is not Ree's favorite." (Writing a cookbook is hard!) But if I were ever to lose my marbles and declare one recipe in this cookbook my favorite, I would be hard-pressed not to choose this one. I first made these little butterscotch cakes on an episode of my cooking show, and we had to close down production for the day because they were so good I could no longer speak. You'll see exactly what I mean when you try these.

Baking spray

8 tablespoons (1 stick) salted butter

¾ cup butterscotch chips

1¼ cups powdered sugar

2 large eggs

3 egg yolks

1 teaspoon vanilla extract

½ cup all-purpose flour

Chocolate ice cream, for serving

1. Preheat the oven to 425°F. Generously spray four ovenproof 6-ounce glass ramekins or custard cups with baking spray and place them on a sheet pan.

2. In a large microwave-safe bowl, combine the butter and butterscotch chips.

3. Microwave them until the butter is melted, about 1 minute. Let it stand for 30 seconds . . .

4. Then whisk until smooth.

5. Sift in the powdered sugar and stir it in.

6. Add the whole eggs and egg yolks and stir them in . . .

7. Then add the vanilla . . .

10. Divide the batter among the four ramekins.

13. And flip the plate over. Carefully remove the ramekin using a hot pad or cloth. Note: This was just at 13 minutes! You can see that the top (which was the bottom) was just barely set. A little more set would be better, but it all worked out in my favor.

8. And the flour . . .

11. Bake until the sides are firm and the centers are soft, 13 to 14 minutes. Let stand for 1 minute (but you want to serve these right away!).

9. And stir it until combined. It's okay if there are a few small lumps!

12. To serve, place an inverted plate on top of a ramekin . . .

14. Carefully place a scoop of ice cream on top and serve immediately. Look at that lava!

MAKE THEM AHEAD!

While lava cakes always need to be baked just before serving (that's why they're so good and gooey!), you can do some steps ahead of time: Make the batter earlier in the day, up to 8 hours before the meal, and store it in the fridge, along with the greased ramekins. Shortly before dinner is ready (about 30 minutes before baking), remove the batter and ramekins from the fridge and let them lose their chill a bit. Then it's just about filling the ramekins and popping them in the oven when you're ready!

CHOCOLATE MINT ICEBOX CAKE

MAKES 8 TO 10 SERVINGS

WHAT: A cool, refreshing cake that gets better as it sits in the icebox (aka fridge!).

WHEN: A backyard summer party or church potluck.

WHY: The ingredient list is short and simple, the assembly is a cinch, and the cake is a dream!

The beauty of icebox cakes, aside from their cool, refreshing tastiness, is the simplicity—not just in the ease of preparation, but also what's in them: This chocolate mint version has a staggering *four ingredients*, which will seem impossible when you taste how wonderful it is.

One 10.1-ounce package Oreo Thins mint chocolate sandwich cookies

1 quart heavy cream

½ teaspoon peppermint extract, or more to taste

1 cup powdered sugar

1. Place one-third of the cookies in a plastic bag. Seal it . . .

3. In the bowl of a stand mixer fitted with the whisk attachment, combine the cream, mint extract, and powdered sugar. Whisk on medium-high speed until stiff.

5. And use a small offset spatula to spread it into an even layer.

2. And crush the cookies with a rolling pin or can until they're broken into pieces. Set aside.

4. Scoop one-third of the whipped cream into a 9-inch springform pan . . .

6. Add half of the whole cookies in a single layer on top of the cream.

7. Repeat with another one-third of the whipped cream and the remaining whole cookies. Top with the remaining whipped cream. (Your layers will look like this: cream, cookies, cream, cookies, cream.)

9. Cover and refrigerate for at least 6 hours, or up to 18 hours. This is the key to an icebox cake!

11. Slice with a sharp knife (the cookies soften while in the fridge, so it's easy!) and serve. It's creamy, chocolate-minty goodness!

8. Pour the crushed cookies on top.

10. Run a small knife around the edge of the pan and release the walls to remove the cake.

Variation

» *Substitute vanilla wafers for the chocolate mint cookies and lemon zest for the mint extract.*

ICEBOX CAKE IDEAS!

With such a simple ingredient list, there's really no limit to the number of icebox cake variations you can come up with. Here's a springboard for your own ideas!

❀ *Gingerbread:* Substitute thin gingersnaps for the chocolate-mint cookies. Stir 1/8 teaspoon ground nutmeg and 1/8 teaspoon ground ginger into the whipped cream.

❀ *Lemon-Basil:* Substitute Meyer lemon Moravian cookie thins for the chocolate-mint cookies. Stir 2 teaspoons lemon zest into the whipped cream. After chilling, decorate the top with pretty basil leaves.

❀ *Pink Lemonade:* Use Oreo Thins lemon sandwich cookies instead of chocolate-mint. Add 2 tablespoons thawed pink lemonade concentrate, 2 teaspoons lemon zest, and a tiny drop of red food coloring to the cream before whipping. Decorate the top with lemon zest before chilling.

❀ *Strawberry Graham:* Use graham crackers instead of chocolate-mint cookies. Add a layer of thinly sliced strawberries on top of each layer of whipped cream. Decorate the top with halved strawberries.

❀ *Tiramisu:* Use any thin vanilla wafer cookie instead of chocolate-mint. Make a simple coffee syrup by combining brewed coffee and sugar. Lightly brush the syrup on each cookie layer. Add 1 teaspoon marsala wine or brandy to the cream before whipping. Top each layer of whipped cream with grated semisweet chocolate.

DESSERT DOUGHNUTS

MAKES ABOUT 18 DOUGHNUTS AND 18 DOUGHNUT HOLES

WHAT: Colorful assorted doughnuts with your choice of sprinkles.

WHEN: When you want to serve a dessert platter that'll wow them!

WHY: Because it's time we all saw doughnuts for the dessert that they are.

I don't know who first proposed that doughnuts—circles of fried dough coated in sugary toppings—were a suitable breakfast, but I'd sure like to party with them and be their friend. And while I'm not above such things, I really like to call things what they are: Doughnuts are dessert! For this fun recipe, I originally considered suggesting store-bought (or even bakery-bought) plain doughnuts and icing and decorating them yourself, and that would work swimmingly . . . but I decided to share my favorite from-scratch doughnut recipe in case you want to go homemade all the way. These are so much fun to make, but even more fun to serve. (Heads up: the dough stays in the fridge overnight, so be sure to plan ahead!)

1. Make the dough: In a small saucepan, combine the milk and sugar and stir over medium-low heat until the sugar is dissolved and the milk reaches 100° to 105°F, about 4 minutes.

2. Remove the pan from the heat. Add the yeast and stir gently. Let sit for 10 minutes.

DOUGHNUTS

1 cup plus 2 tablespoons whole milk

¼ cup sugar

1 package (2¼ teaspoons) active dry yeast

2 large eggs, beaten

10 tablespoons (1¼ sticks) butter, melted

4 cups all-purpose flour, plus more for rolling out the dough

¼ teaspoon kosher salt

Oil, for the bowl

About 2½ pounds lard or 6 cups peanut oil, for deep-frying

GLAZE

1¼ cups powdered sugar, sifted

2 tablespoons whole milk

1 to 4 drops bright food coloring

TOPPINGS

Rainbow sprinkles

Chocolate jimmies

Graham crackers, crushed

Oreos, broken into pieces

Mini chocolate chips

GANACHE

6 ounces semisweet chocolate, chopped

⅓ cup heavy cream, heated to a simmer

3. Pour the eggs into the bowl of a stand mixer fitted with the dough hook attachment.

4. Turn the mixer on medium-low and add the melted butter . . .

5. The milk and yeast mixture . . .

6. And the flour and salt. Mix on medium speed until the dough comes together, then continue to let it mix/knead for 10 minutes.

7. Transfer the dough to a lightly oiled bowl. Turn the dough to coat, then cover the bowl with plastic wrap and refrigerate for 8 hours or overnight.

8. When you're ready to make the doughnuts, remove the plastic wrap and let the dough sit on the counter for 20 minutes.

9. Turn out the dough onto a lightly floured surface. Roll the dough out to ¼-inch thickness.

10. Using a doughnut cutter, cut out as many rounds as you can.

11. Separate the rounds from the holes and place them on a sheet pan. Cover them with a lightweight kitchen towel and place them in a draft-free place in the kitchen . . .

12. Until they are risen and puffy, about 1½ hours.

13. Add enough lard to a large Dutch oven to come up 4 inches. Heat the lard over medium heat until a deep-frying thermometer registers 360°F. Carefully lower the doughnuts into the oil in batches, 4 or 5 at a time . . .

14. Gently turning them to brown evenly. Each batch should take 2 to 2½ minutes to brown on both sides.

18. Then turn them over, place them on a cooling rack over a sheet pan, and immediately add your toppings of choice.

21. Keep going until you have a super-fun variety, dipping in the glaze or ganache and sprinkling on the fun!

15. Remove the doughnuts to a pan lined with paper towels.

19. Don't be afraid to do more than one color!

The possibilities are endless.

16. Keep going until everything is fried and crisp!

20. For chocolate-iced doughnuts, make a ganache: In a bowl, combine the chocolate and warmed cream and let sit for a couple of minutes. When the chocolate has started to soften, whisk it slowly until smooth (see page 327). Dip the doughnuts in the same way and add your toppings. Note that the ganache will be a little thicker than the glaze!

Psst. Don't forget the holes!

17. Make a colorful glaze: In a bowl, mix together the powdered sugar, milk, and food coloring. Dip the doughnuts until they are halfway submerged . . .

CARAMEL PECAN CHEESECAKES

MAKES 12 MUFFIN-SIZE CHEESECAKES

WHAT: Individual cheesecakes with caramel, chocolate, and pecans.

WHEN: Office parties, potlucks, snacks.

WHY: They're cute and irresistible! Emphasis on addictive.

Turtles candies are a favorite in the ol' Drummond household, and bags (or boxes . . . or truckloads) of them will disappear faster than dead winter grass in a spring prairie fire. The salty-sweet combination of chocolate, caramel, and pecans is simply divine, and these little round cheesecakes satisfy even the strongest Turtles cravers among us. On another note, wouldn't that make the best title for a rock band? The Turtles Cravers! I'd buy a ticket to that concert.

1. Preheat the oven to 350°F. Line twelve cups of a standard muffin tin with paper liners.

2. First, make the crust: Break the graham crackers into squares and place in a food processor.

4. Then pulse the crackers . . .

3. Add the sugar . . .

5. Until they're really fine crumbs.

CRUST

12 chocolate graham crackers (the large rectangles)

¼ cup sugar

4 tablespoons (½ stick) salted butter, melted

FILLING

12 ounces cream cheese, at room temperature

½ cup sugar

1 large egg

½ teaspoon vanilla extract

¼ cup caramel sauce, store-bought or homemade (see page 332)

GANACHE

6 ounces semisweet chocolate, chopped

⅓ cup heavy cream, heated just to a simmer

TOPPINGS

12 pecan halves

3 tablespoons mini chocolate chips

3 tablespoons caramel sauce, store-bought or homemade

6. Keep pulsing while you drizzle in the melted butter.

10. Now just set these aside; no need to bake 'em!

14. And vanilla.

7. Then pulse a few more times, until the crumbs are nice and moist.

11. Next up, make the filling: Add the softened cream cheese to the bowl of a stand mixer fitted with the paddle attachment.

15. Beat until totally smooth.

8. Place 2 tablespoons of crumbs in each lined muffin cup.

12. Add the sugar . . .

16. Drizzle in the caramel sauce . . .

9. Use the bottom of a ¼-cup measure to pack the crumbs tightly in the cups.

13. Egg . . .

17. And mix it in, scraping the sides of the bowl once midway.

18. Divide the batter equally among the muffin cups and bake for 17 minutes.

19. Let them cool for a bit, then chill in the fridge for at least 2 hours or overnight.

20. When the cheesecakes are chilled, make the ganache: Place the semisweet chocolate in a bowl and pour the warmed cream on top.

21. Let sit for a couple of minutes. When the chocolate has started to soften, start whisking it slowly . . .

22. And keep going until the mixture is smooth and perfect. Note: This is a slightly thick ganache.

23. Add about a tablespoon of the ganache to the top of each cheesecake and spread to even it out.

24. Lightly press a pecan half in the center of each little cake . . .

25. Then sprinkle mini chocolate chips all over . . .

26. And finally, drizzle on a little caramel sauce.

27. You can freeze these in the finished form, then just pull them out and let them thaw. Or you can chill them in the fridge and serve them later in the day.

PRESTO CHANGE-O!

Turn the caramel pecan version into a peanut butter cup version by spiking the cheesecake mixture with 2 tablespoons of peanut butter instead of caramel. Then, instead of pecan halves, decorate the top of each with a halved peanut butter cup and a sprinkling of mini chocolate chips.

STRAWBERRY SPRINKLE CHEESECAKES

MAKES 12 MUFFIN-SIZE CHEESECAKES

WHAT: Individual cheesecakes with strawberries and sprinkles.

WHEN: A sweet treat on your own, or a pretty dessert for any occasion.

WHY: They're red, pretty, and sparkly. Case closed!

I love cheesecake as much as the next person, but a whole, regular-size cheesecake can be such a commitment, and even then, you're never assured that you'll wind up with a good one that doesn't have a huge crack down the middle! These muffin-size cheesecakes are the perfect solution, and you can keep them in the fridge for up to a week, grabbing one (or two) as the situation dictates. You can change up the fruit and sprinkle color to fit your fancy, which makes this recipe a great one for any season or party. You'll be hooked!

1. Preheat the oven to 350°F. Line twelve cups of a standard muffin tin with paper liners.

2. Break the graham crackers into squares and place them in a food processor, then add the sugar.

3. Pulse them as you drizzle the melted butter into the machine . . .

4. Until they're broken up into fine crumbs.

5. Add about 2 tablespoons of the crumbs to a muffin cup and press with the bottom of a metal ¼-cup measure to pack tightly. Repeat with the rest of the muffin cups.

CRUST

12 graham crackers (the large rectangles)

¼ cup sugar

4 tablespoons (½ stick) salted butter, melted

FILLING

12 ounces cream cheese, at room temperature

½ cup sugar

1 large egg

½ teaspoon vanilla extract

2 tablespoons plus ½ cup strawberry preserves

GANACHE

6 ounces white chocolate, roughly chopped

⅓ cup heavy cream, heated just to a simmer

TOPPINGS

6 strawberries, halved (the prettier the better)

Red sugar sprinkles

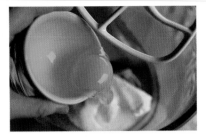

6. Make the filling: In the bowl of a stand mixer fitted with the paddle attachment, combine the cream cheese, sugar, and egg. Turn the speed to low.

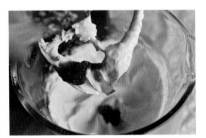

7. Add the vanilla, and continue beating until smooth, scraping once during the process.

8. Add 2 tablespoons of the strawberry preserves . . .

9. And mix until combined.

10. Spread 2 teaspoons strawberry preserves on top of each crust, spreading to cover.

11. Distribute the batter among the muffin tins, tapping the bottom of the tin lightly on the counter to help the batter settle.

12. Bake until set in the center, just 17 minutes. Cool on a wire rack, then chill for at least 2 hours and up to 24 hours.

13. Place the white chocolate in a bowl and pour the hot cream over it. Let it sit for 2 minutes.

14. Whisk or stir slowly until the chocolate is totally melted and the mixture is smooth.

15. Spoon a generous tablespoon of the ganache on top of each cheesecake . . .

16. Then top with a strawberry half, cut side down, and add the sprinkles! Chill until serving.

Note: Because of the fresh strawberry on top, it's best to serve these within 12 hours.

CARAMEL APPLE QUESADILLAS

MAKES FOUR 10-INCH QUESADILLAS (TO SERVE 8)

WHAT: Sweet cinnamon-y apple slices in a cream cheese and caramel quesadilla. You heard me.

WHEN: Snack, post-meal dessert, midnight treat for two.

WHY: Because it takes way longer to make a caramel apple pie.

I'm not entirely sure what took me so long to get hip to the fact that quesadillas can be turned into a sweet treat, but oh, brother (and sister), they can. And I believe in putting as much care and detail into a sweet quesadilla as I would a savory one. As such, I am not content to merely slap some peanut butter in between two tortillas, grill it, and call it good. I love a mix of flavors and ingredients and textures and degrees of sin. Read on; all will become clear!

8 tablespoons (1 stick) salted butter

1 cup plus 2 tablespoons packed brown sugar

1 tablespoon vanilla extract

½ cup buttermilk (see Note)

Pinch of kosher salt

½ cup granulated sugar

1 teaspoon ground cinnamon

8 ounces cream cheese, at room temperature

8 burrito-size whole wheat tortillas

3 Granny Smith apples, cored and very thinly sliced (reserve about 12 slices for garnish)

4 tablespoons finely chopped pecans

Unsweetened whipped cream, for serving

1. In a medium skillet, combine 4 tablespoons (½ stick) of the butter and 1 cup of the brown sugar and set over medium-low heat.

4. And let it bubble up gently. Cook, stirring occasionally, until thickened, about 5 minutes. Remove the caramel sauce from the heat and set it aside to cool slightly.

7. And smush it together until smooth.

2. Add the vanilla, then stir as it starts to cook and dissolve.

5. In a small bowl, mix together the granulated sugar and cinnamon. Set it aside.

8. Spread a tortilla with one-quarter of the cream cheese mixture.

3. Stir in the buttermilk and salt . . .

6. In a separate medium bowl, combine the cream cheese with the remaining 2 tablespoons brown sugar . . .

9. Lay apple slices all over the cream cheese . . .

10. And sprinkle on some of the cinnamon sugar and 1 tablespoon of the chopped pecans.

13. Then flip the quesadilla and let it brown on the other side, another minute or two. Set aside and repeat to assemble and cook the other 3 quesadillas.

16. Serve a few wedges with a dollop of (preferably unsweetened) whipped cream, extra apple slices, and more caramel sauce!

11. Heat a large cast-iron skillet over medium-low heat and add 1 tablespoon of the butter. Lay the filled tortilla in the skillet . . .

14. Remove the quesadillas to a board, cut them into wedges, and sprinkle on more cinnamon sugar.

And one other thing: *Gosh, these are good!*

Note: If you don't have buttermilk, just measure a little less than ½ cup regular milk, then top it off with distilled white vinegar to reach ½ cup. Let it stand for 5 minutes and stir. Buttermilk!

Then top with a second tortilla. Let the bottom tortilla cook for a couple of minutes . . .

12. Then top with a second tortilla. Let the bottom tortilla cook for a couple of minutes . . .

15. Transfer the caramel sauce to a pitcher and pour it in a swirl over the top.

Variations

» *Use sliced pears or peaches instead of apples.*

» *To save a step, use good-quality jarred caramel sauce instead of homemade.*

» *Omit the caramel sauce and use Nutella instead.*

» *Use both caramel and Nutella!*

FAST AND FRUITY NO-CHURN ICE CREAM

MAKES ABOUT 1 QUART

WHAT: A lower-sugar, lower-carb, creamy-delicious treat!

WHEN: When you've gotta have ice cream. (It happens to me daily.)

WHY: Because you don't have to churn it! And it's soooo good.

I've enjoyed dabbling in and out of the lower-carb lifestyle, and when I'm all in, I so enjoy this creamy, lower-sugar alternative to regular ice cream. There are many things to love about it, not the least of which is how quick and easy it is to make. You can have an ice cream craving one minute, and within 7 or 8 minutes, you can have a cold, refreshing bowl of ice cream in your hot little hands. (Just make sure they aren't too hot. You don't want it to melt!)

Nothing could ever substitute for the real thing . . . but this will make you feel less alone when you're trying to step away from the sugar.

3 ounces semisweet or bittersweet chocolate, plus more for shaving

2 cups frozen mango, unthawed

2 cups frozen strawberries, unthawed

1 cup very cold plain whole-milk Greek yogurt

½ cup very cold heavy cream

2 tablespoons honey

1½ teaspoons vanilla extract

Ice cream without the guilt!

1. Chop the chocolate and set it aside.

2. Place the frozen fruit in a food processor.

3. Add the yogurt, cream, honey, and vanilla . . .

4. And pulse and process until the mixture is creamy and the fruit is all broken up.

5. Add the chocolate . . .

6. And pulse until the chocolate is mostly broken up into bits. It should be very thick!

7. Immediately scoop the ice cream into a bowl . . .

8. And shave more chocolate on top. This has a nice soft-serve consistency . . .

9. But for a firmer ice cream, scoop onto a sheet pan lined with parchment and freeze until hard.

This is mine. Where's yours?

Variations

» *Use any combination of frozen fruit you'd like!*

» *For those of you who can stand to eat bananas (and I am not one of them), I hear a frozen banana can add a nice creaminess. (Yuck. But go for it if you'd like. But yuck.)*

» *Add a couple packets of artificial sweetener if you like.*

CHOCOLATE DEVILS

MAKES 12 DEVILS

WHAT: Chocolate cake sandwiches with a light cream filling and ganache.

WHEN: Birthday parties, baby showers, Valentine's Day!

WHY: Because . . . um . . . look at it. Such a delicious, chocolaty treat.

Suzy-Qs, Devil Dogs, Chocolate Devils . . . they're all cut from the same cloth. The first two are store-bought treats, but the last one? You can make them at home yourself! Granted, there are approximately four thousand steps to these, but none of them are complicated at all. To simplify: It's cake. The best white frosting you'll ever taste. A rich ganache. And a cherry. Case closed!

Butter, for the pan

1. Preheat the oven to 350°F. Generously grease a 13 x 18-inch sheet pan with butter.

2. Make the cake: In a large bowl, stir together the flour, sugar, and salt.

3. In a medium saucepan, melt the butter over medium heat. Stir in the cocoa powder.

4. Pour in the boiling water . . .

5. Then let the mixture come to a gentle boil.

CAKE

2 cups all-purpose flour

2 cups sugar

¼ teaspoon kosher salt

1 cup (2 sticks) salted butter

4 heaping tablespoons unsweetened cocoa powder

1 cup boiling water

½ cup buttermilk (see Note, page 333)

2 large eggs

1 teaspoon baking soda

1 teaspoon vanilla extract

WHITE FROSTING

1 cup whole milk

5 tablespoons all-purpose flour

1 cup (2 sticks) salted butter, softened

1 cup sugar

1 teaspoon vanilla extract .

GANACHE AND GARNISH

24 ounces semisweet chips

1⅓ cups heavy cream

2 teaspoons vanilla extract

12 maraschino cherries

6. Pour the chocolate mixture into the flour mixture . . .

7. And stir until halfway combined. Set aside.

8. In a small pitcher, whisk the buttermilk, eggs, baking soda, and vanilla.

9. Pour the buttermilk mixture into the chocolate-flour mixture . . .

10. And fold together until combined.

11. Pour the batter into the prepared sheet pan.

12. Bake until set in the very center, about 20 minutes. Let cool completely.

13. While the cake is cooling, make the white frosting: In a large saucepan, combine the milk and flour . . .

14. And cook over medium heat, whisking gently, until the mixture becomes very thick. Remove from the heat and let cool to room temperature.

15. Meanwhile, in the bowl of a stand mixer fitted with the paddle attachment, cream the butter and sugar until light and fluffy, about 3 minutes.

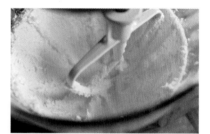

16. Add the vanilla and mix it in.

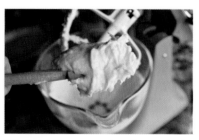

17. Add the completely cooled milk and flour mixture . . .

18. And beat the living daylights out of it for at least 5 minutes, scraping a couple of times during the process. (You won't believe how good this is!)

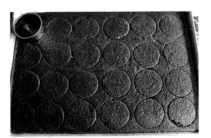

19. When the cake is cooled, use a 2-inch round cutter to cut out twenty-four rounds. Carefully remove the cake rounds to another sheet pan with a cooling rack set inside. (You're the baker, so you get to eat the cake scraps!)

20. Put the frosting in a pastry bag fitted with a large star tip. (Or you can just spread it with an offset spatula!) Squeeze a generous round of frosting on twelve of the cake rounds . . .

21. And top them with the other twelve rounds.

22. Make the ganache: Place the chocolate chips in a large bowl. In a medium saucepan, heat the cream over medium-low heat until very hot (but don't let it boil). Add the vanilla, then pour the mixture over the chocolate chips.

23. Let sit for a minute, then stir to melt the chips completely.

24. Spoon ganache over each sandwich, letting it drip down the sides.

25. Then top with the cherries!

26. Chill until serving, or dig in immediately. (I recommend the latter!) These will keep in the fridge for up to 3 days.

VANILLA BEAN MERINGUE COOKIES

MAKES ABOUT 24 COOKIES

WHAT: Light, airy cookies that taste like clouds.
WHEN: A midday sweet treat, a fancy cookie for a party, or a little goodie before bed.
WHY: Because they serve these cookies in Heaven!

Meringue cookies are gluten-free—not a touch of flour anywhere—but that's not why I love them. I love them because they're pretty and sweet, and because their texture completely fascinates me. They're like eating cute little fluffy clouds, if you could even eat clouds, but little *crisp* fluffy clouds, if clouds could even be crisp . . . if that makes sense at all. As I have just demonstrated, meringue cookies are hard to describe to someone who hasn't tried them. So if you fit into that category, please try them! Then we can be fascinated together. Note: It can be difficult to keep meringue cookies crisp in very humid environments. So these are best in cooler weather or in air-conditioning!

3 large egg whites, at room temperature	1 vanilla bean ⅛ teaspoon cream of tartar	¾ cup sugar

1. Preheat the oven to 200°F. Line two sheet pans with parchment.

2. Pour the egg whites into the bowl of a stand mixer fitted with the whisk attachment.

3. Use a paring knife to split the vanilla bean down the center, then run the back of the knife down the center to scrape out the caviar.

4. Add the caviar and cream of tartar to the egg whites . . .

5. And beat on medium-high until the mixture is frothy and soft peaks form, about 2 minutes. Reduce the speed to medium and continue to beat, adding the sugar 1 tablespoon at a time and waiting about 15 seconds between additions.

6. When all the sugar has been added, continue beating on medium for 5 minutes, until very stiff and glossy!

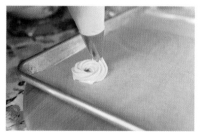

7. Spoon the meringue into a large pastry bag fitted with a #6 star tip, then pipe the meringue in a neat little circle on the parchment . . .

8. Ending with a little peak in the center.

9. Continue piping, leaving a good 1 inch between the cookies. (If you don't want to use a pastry bag, you can use two spoons to add drops of the meringue, much like you'd add drops of regular cookie dough to a pan.)

10. Repeat with the rest of the meringue on a second pan. Bake for 1 hour, then turn off the oven and leave the cookies in the oven for 45 minutes. Remove them from the oven and let cool completely. Store in an airtight container.

I repeat: I'm fascinated.

PEANUT BUTTER-STUFFED CHOCOLATE CHUNK COOKIES

MAKES 18 COOKIES

WHAT: Delicious chocolate chunk cookies with ooey-gooey peanut butter filling.

WHEN: When you want to take your cookie life to the next level! (Todd and Bryce love these more than their football cleats.)

WHY: Because they're "two great tastes that taste great together." (Sound familiar?)

Those classic peanut butter/Hershey's Kiss cookies are among the handful of cookie varieties that render me completely incapable of practicing self-control. There's something about those warm peanut butter cookies with that softened chocolate kiss on top that just drives me batty in the most wonderful way. These luscious stuffed cookies are sort of a deconstructed, then put back together and turned upside down, take on those beloved cookies from my youth.

Gooey goodness!

1 cup smooth peanut butter

½ cup powdered sugar

8 tablespoons (1 stick) salted butter, softened

⅔ cup packed brown sugar

¼ cup granulated sugar

1 teaspoon vanilla extract

1 large egg

1½ cups all-purpose flour

½ teaspoon baking soda

½ teaspoon baking powder

½ teaspoon kosher salt

1 heaping teaspoon instant coffee granules

4 ounces good-quality semisweet chocolate, chopped into chunks

1. In a medium bowl, combine the peanut butter and powdered sugar . . .

2. And mix with a spatula until smooth.

3. Using a tablespoon scoop, portion into eighteen rounds onto a parchment-lined pan. Place the pan in the freezer to firm up while you make the cookie dough.

4. In the bowl of a stand mixer fitted with the paddle attachment, cream together the butter, brown sugar, and granulated sugar.

5. Add the vanilla and egg, then mix on medium speed until smooth, about 2 minutes. Scrape the bowl and mix again.

6. In a separate bowl, combine the flour, baking soda, baking powder, salt, and coffee granules. Stir together.

7. Add the flour mixture to the mixer in two batches, mixing on low until totally incorporated.

8. Add the chocolate chunks and mix on low.

9. Scoop the cookie dough into 18 portions (about 2 tablespoons each) onto another parchment-lined sheet pan . . .

10. And flatten each scoop into a disc.

11. Remove the scooped peanut butter rounds from the freezer. They should be firm and cold but not hard.

12. Place a peanut butter round on the center of each dough round.

13. Bring the edges of the dough around the peanut butter and enclose it completely . . .

14. Then use your fingers to seal the dough around the peanut butter and form the cookie into a disc.

15. When all of the cookies are made, distribute them between the two baking sheets and refrigerate for 20 minutes.

16. Meanwhile, preheat the oven to 375°F.

17. Bake the cookies until golden brown, 10 to 11 minutes. Remove the cookies from the oven and transfer them to a cooling rack.

18. The center will be hot, so let them cool slightly before eating, about 5 minutes. Note that as the cookies cool, the peanut butter filling will become more solid. You can warm the cookies in the microwave for 10 to 15 seconds to soften them as needed!

11-CARTON CAKE

MAKES 8 TO 10 SERVINGS

WHAT: A moist and marvelous chocolate cake that makes measuring a cinch.

WHEN: Birthday, potluck—any time you need a one-layer cake in your life.

WHY: Because you can tell yourself the yogurt was a healthy choice!

Yogurt pot cakes were invented in France, and they make clever use of a yogurt container; it becomes the measuring cup for some of the other cake ingredients! They're fun!

CAKE

Baking spray

One 6-ounce carton vanilla yogurt (save the empty carton for measuring the rest of the ingredients)

One 6-ounce carton vegetable oil

One 6-ounce carton granulated sugar

2 large eggs, at room temperature

Two 6-ounce cartons cake flour

½ teaspoon baking soda

½ teaspoon baking powder

One 6-ounce carton unsweetened cocoa powder

1½ teaspoons vanilla extract

One 6-ounce carton whole milk

One 6-ounce carton semisweet mini chocolate chips

VANILLA BUTTERCREAM FROSTING

12 tablespoons (1½ sticks) salted butter, softened

Two 6-ounce cartons powdered sugar

½ teaspoon vanilla extract

One 6-ounce carton semisweet mini chocolate chips

1. Position a rack in the middle of the oven and preheat it to 350°F. Generously spray a 10-inch round cake pan with baking spray.

2. Empty the yogurt into a large bowl, scraping the carton as clean as possible.

This is now your measuring cup!

3. Add the oil . . .

4. The sugar and the eggs . . .

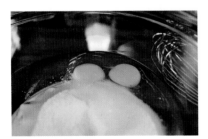

5. And whisk well to combine.

6. Measure one carton of flour. Add the baking soda and baking powder and stir.

7. Add the flour mixture along with the second carton of flour to the wet ingredients . . .

8. Then add the cocoa powder and stir.

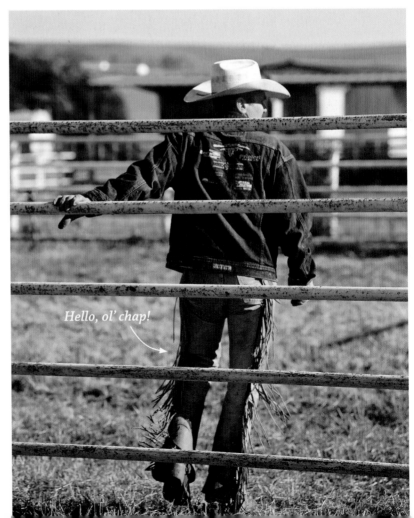

Hello, ol' chap!

9. Add the vanilla and the milk . . .

10. And stir to combine. Stir in the mini chocolate chips! This is getting exciting!

11. Pour the batter into the prepared cake pan.

12. Bake until a toothpick inserted into the center of the cake comes out clean, 35 to 38 minutes.

13. Let the cake cool in the pan for 5 minutes, then remove the cake from the pan and place it on a rack to cool.

14. Make the vanilla buttercream frosting: In the bowl of a stand mixer fitted with the paddle attachment, combine the butter, powdered sugar, and vanilla . . .

15. Then mix it until it's totally smooth, scraping the sides once or twice during the process.

16. When the cake is completely cool, plop the frosting on . . .

17. And spread it all over the top . . .

18. Then sprinkle with the chocolate chips.

19. Slice, slice, baby!

A zero-calorie treat! Just kidding.

FUNNEL CAKE SUNDAES

MAKES FOUR 10-INCH FUNNEL CAKE SUNDAES

WHAT: Crispy, golden-fried funnel cakes topped with ice cream and fixins.

WHEN: Slumber parties, birthday parties, Wednesdays.

WHY: Because it's one of the most ridonculous desserts you'll ever eat, and it'll command the attention of the room! Even if you're the only one in the room.

I still marvel that there are actually some Americans who have never heard of, let alone eaten, a funnel cake. To me, they're the most iconic carnival/amusement park goodie there is—one of the truly great comfort treats that instantly transports you back to your childhood. A funnel cake on its own (with just a sprinkling of powdered sugar) is perfection enough, but if you use it as a base for an ice cream sundae, it's an indulgent mash-up of such epic proportions that it will most certainly wind up on your "I can have one of these a year, max" list. (My list is 365 items long . . .)

1½ cups all-purpose flour

2 tablespoons sugar

1 teaspoon baking powder

Pinch of kosher salt

1¼ cups whole milk

1 large egg

½ teaspoon vanilla extract

2 tablespoons salted butter, melted

Vegetable oil, for deep-frying

Powdered sugar, for dusting

12 scoops ice cream (I used rocky road, cherry, and caramel)

½ cup hot fudge sauce

Rainbow sprinkles, for serving

Whipped cream, for serving

Maraschino cherries, for serving

1. In a large measuring pitcher, whisk the flour, sugar, baking powder, and salt.

3. Add the egg and vanilla . . .

5. Pour in the melted butter and whisk it in.

2. Pour in the milk.

4. And whisk until smooth.

6. Pour 3 inches of vegetable oil into a large, heavy pot and heat over medium-high heat until a deep-frying thermometer registers 350°F. (Place the pot on the back burner if you have children in the house!)

7. Use your index finger to stop up the end of a metal funnel . . .

8. While you grasp the top of the funnel with your thumb. Make one funnel cake at a time: Pour ¾ cup of the batter into the funnel, keeping the bottom plugged with your finger.

9. Carefully move the funnel over to the oil and let the batter flow out, moving the funnel around to swirl the batter and create the funnel cake. *Important: Keep the end of the funnel no more than an inch or two away from the surface of the oil or the batter will disperse rather than come together.*

10. Let the funnel cake fry and brown for about 1½ minutes on the first side, using a metal spider or spatula to gently move it around in the oil. Very carefully turn the funnel cake over, using a second spatula if necessary to keep the oil from splashing.

11. When it's golden on the second side . . .

12. Transfer it to a plate lined with paper towels to drain. Repeat with the remaining batter.

13. Place the funnel cakes on dessert plates and dust them with powdered sugar.

14. Top them with the ice cream, hot fudge, sprinkles, whipped cream, and cherries!

Variation

›› *Omit the ice cream and fixins and just enjoy the funnel cake with powdered sugar!*

CONFETTI CAKE

MAKES ONE 8-INCH 3-LAYER CAKE (TO SERVE 8 TO 10)

WHAT: A bountiful three-layer celebration cake with colorful "confetti" sprinkles.

WHEN: Birthday, graduation, or any special occasion.

WHY: Because this cake results in oohs, aahs, and smiles across the board. I've seen it happen!

When it comes to cakes, I'm absolutely a quick-and-easy kind of gal. When we celebrate birthdays or other milestones in the Drummond family, a chocolate sheet cake is almost always our treat of choice, and I'm happy for that to be the extent of my personal cake narrative in the ongoing story of my life. However, there are times every once in a great while when a gal has to push the boundaries of her cake narrative and whip out a big, beautiful layer cake with rainbow sprinkles and Swiss buttercream frosting! This is a lovely recipe, one that takes a million years to make, but it's actually a lot of fun . . . and when you remove that first slice, it will all make perfect sense.

1. Preheat the oven to 350°F. Butter three 8-inch round cake pans and line the bottoms with rounds of parchment paper. Butter the parchment, then dust with flour, shaking out the excess.

2. In the bowl of a stand mixer fitted with the paddle attachment, combine the softened butter and sugar . . .

3. And beat on medium speed until the mixture is pale yellow and fluffy, about 4 minutes.

4. Reduce the mixer speed to medium-low, then add the egg whites in about 4 additions, allowing them to incorporate after each addition.

CAKE

Butter and flour, for the pans

1½ cups (3 sticks) unsalted butter, softened

2¼ cups sugar

6 large egg whites

2 tablespoons vanilla extract

1½ cups all-purpose flour

2¾ cups cake flour

1 tablespoon plus ¼ teaspoon baking powder

1 teaspoon table salt

1½ cups whole milk

1 cup plus 2 tablespoons rainbow sprinkles

FROSTING

8 large egg whites

2 cups sugar

3 cups (6 sticks) unsalted butter, cut into pats, softened

1 tablespoon vanilla extract

Pinch of table salt

2 to 3 tablespoons sprinkles, for decorating

5. Scrape down the sides of the bowl with a rubber spatula . . .

6. Then add the vanilla . . .

7. And beat for 1 more minute.

8. In a separate large bowl, whisk the all-purpose flour, cake flour, baking powder, and salt.

9. Turn the speed to low and add one-third of the flour mixture, beating until it is just mixed in.

10. Pour in one-third of the milk and beat until incorporated.

11. Continue alternating the flour mixture and the milk two more times, until all the dry ingredients and milk have been incorporated. Stop mixing just after it's all combined.

12. Add the sprinkles . . .

13. And mix on low for about 5 seconds, just until the sprinkles are mixed in. Fold the batter with a rubber spatula if necessary to mix them in more.

14. Divide the batter evenly among the three pans.

15. Bake until the cakes are golden on the surface and a toothpick inserted into the center comes out clean, 23 to 25 minutes. Let them cool in the pans for 15 minutes, then carefully invert the pans and set the cakes aside to cool completely. Peel the parchment from the bottom of the layers.

16. Make the frosting: Set a large heatproof bowl over a pan of simmering water. Place the egg whites and sugar in the bowl.

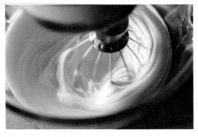

19. Now this is where it gets fun! Whisk the mixture on medium speed for 5 minutes . . .

22. Turn the mixer speed to medium-low, then add the butter in batches, about 3 tablespoons at a time, beating well after each addition. This will take a while, but it's worth the time!

17. Whisk until the sugar is completely dissolved and the mixture is very warm, about 3 minutes.

20. Then increase the mixer to medium-high and whip until stiff and glossy, about 7 more minutes.

23. Add the vanilla and salt and beat on medium speed for another 4 minutes, until fluffy.

18. Transfer the mixture to the bowl of a stand mixer fitted with the whisk attachment.

21. Important! The mixer bowl should no longer be warm to the touch. If it is, you can wait a few minutes before proceeding, or you can hold a towel filled with ice on the bottom for a couple of minutes. (This will keep the butter from melting when you put it in.)

24. Smear a little of the frosting on a cake platter or cake stand.

25. Place one layer of cake upside down on the stand (trim the underside to be flat if it's too mounded). Spread about 1½ cups of the frosting all over the surface, extending the frosting out to beyond the edge.

26. Repeat this two more times.

27. Use a dinner knife or offset spatula to spread the remaining frosting all over the surface of the cake, pushing a little extra into any gaps between layers. You can do a textured/peaked surface, or you can make it perfectly smooth (I settled a little in the middle!).

28. Cover the top of the cake with sprinkles . . .

29. . . . And slice the cake into wedges. It'll make everyone happy!

Note: Because of the amount of butter in the frosting, the cake should be stored in the fridge. Just remove it from the fridge and let it sit at room temperature for 30 minutes before slicing and serving.

SPRINKLE NUMBERS

Personalize your cake with an age or a name!

1. Gently place cookie cutters on the surface of the cake . . .

2. And carefully spoon in the sprinkles. Tiny nonpareils work best!

3. Use your finger to reach inside and even them out, then steadily lift off the cutters.

Acknowledgments

So many people to thank, so little paper! But I'm going to do my best, because I love you all.

First, to *you*. Whether this is your first time buying one of my cookbooks or you're adding to your collection, I can't thank you enough for your love and support. I feel it daily, and I certainly felt it during the long days of cooking and writing. Thank you so much, friends.

To Haley Carter, my assistant and friend. I can't begin to thank you for the help you provide me daily! I'm so glad our Myers-Briggs types are the perfect match. So proud of you.

To Trey Wilson, Tiffany Taylor, and Matt Taylor, my beyond-perfect cookbook team! Between you guys and Haley, this cookbook was by far the most enjoyable yet. You made everything so fun, so seamless, and most important, you kept the yacht rock flowing. Thank you so much for sharing your time and talents with me!

To Cassie Jones Morgan, the Greatest Editor of All Time. If cookbooks were children, I'd have more kids with you than my own husband! I can't imagine going through this process with anyone else. If you leave me, I'm coming with you.

To Kris Tobiassen, for your amazing design talents. You made this cookbook extra fun!

To Susanna Einstein, Anwesha Basu, Liate Stehlik, Kara Zauberman, Tavia Kowalchuk, Rachel Meyers, and Anna Brower for all your support and help. I appreciate you so much!

To my beautiful friends who mean so much to me—there are too many to name, but you know who you are. I love you all.

To my family, for being there.

To my children, for being my heart.

To Ladd, for everything.

Universal Conversion chart

OVEN TEMPERATURE EQUIVALENTS

250°F = 120°C
275°F = 135°C
300°F = 150°C
325°F = 160°C
350°F = 180°C
375°F = 190°C
400°F = 200°C
425°F = 220°C
450°F = 230°C
475°F = 240°C
500°F = 260°C

MEASUREMENT EQUIVALENTS

Measurements should always be level unless directed otherwise.

⅛ teaspoon = 0.5 mL
¼ teaspoon = 1 mL
½ teaspoon = 2 mL
1 teaspoon = 5 mL
1 tablespoon = 3 teaspoons = ½ fluid ounce = 15 mL
2 tablespoons = ⅛ cup = 1 fluid ounce = 30 mL
4 tablespoons = ¼ cup = 2 fluid ounces = 60 mL
5⅓ tablespoons = ⅓ cup = 3 fluid ounces = 80 mL
8 tablespoons = ½ cup = 4 fluid ounces = 120 mL
10⅔ tablespoons = ⅔ cup = 5 fluid ounces = 160 mL
12 tablespoons = ¾ cup = 6 fluid ounces = 180 mL
16 tablespoons = 1 cup = 8 fluid ounces = 240 mL

Index

The End
Walter needs a nap!